To Debbie,

with warm regards
- thanks for being at this
conference.

Leon W. [signature]

the
INNOCENCE
of GOD

the INNOCENCE *of* GOD

UDO MIDDELMANN

Paternoster:
thinking faith

COLORADO SPRINGS · LONDON · HYDERABAD

Paternoster Publishing

We welcome your questions and comments.

USA   1820 Jet Stream Drive, Colorado Springs, CO 80921
       www.authenticbooks.com

UK   9 Holdom Avenue, Bletchley, Milton Keynes, Bucks, MK1 1QR
       www.authenticmedia.co.uk

India Logos Bhavan, Medchal Road, Jeedimetla Village, Secunderabad
       500 055, A.P.

The Innocence of God

ISBN-13: 978-1-934068-04-5

ISBN-10: 1-934068-04-7

Cover design: Paul Lewis

Interior design: Angela Lewis

Editorial team: Mike Morrell, KJ Larson, Betsy Weinrich

Printed in the United States of America

Contents

To Deborah, still and always,

now with five "living books" between us

our children

Natasha, Samantha, Naomi, Hannah, Isaac

INTRODUCTION

The barber up the road has lived long enough to reject any belief or even interest in God. For him, the reality of a painful world is enough evidence to conclude that there is no god worth seeking. The twentieth century's global inhumanities have rubbed salt into wounds that should have long since been healed. Nothing has really improved in a world where human evil and natural catastrophes have teamed up to produce enormous suffering, seeming more the norm than the exception. All religion has ever done is pretend to have an answer. But these "answers" have often kept people from doing anything proactive in response, since in some way God or gods are responsible for it all.

Too bad that Christians have often joined this chorus! The barber never heard anything else but that a God is in charge whose weakness is somehow his strength; a deity who demands a spiritual maturity from us to accept stoically all that happens. Funeral notices announce that "it is God's will to take home to himself" the deceased. Common Christian parlance makes God the power that defines and demands faith, exploiting people's need to worship something. Even insurance companies still use the phrase "act of God" to describe liability when no one else can be charged.

With all we know today about history, humanity, and global culture, it is easier to conclude that God does not exist and that people of faith are fools. Reality is such a mess. If there is a God in charge of this, God should be held accountable for a monstrous experience. More often, such belief in a God "out there" is passé, a relic from eras when people needed explanations to hold together the horror of the many contradictory experiences in their lives. Someone in heaven must be behind all this, in the same way that there was always some evil ruler behind everything bad on earth. In the past people believed from fear, just as political fear silenced most opposition to dictators. Fast-forward to today: We fear being taken for a ride by religion. The only thing that seems credible to believe in, in twenty-first-century life, is ourselves.

"I have never believed in God. Not in *your* God anyway, the one who looks down onto his chessboard and moves the pieces according to his pleasure, occasionally glancing up at the face of his Adversary with the smile of one who already knows the outcome. At least the Devil plays fair! We know where he stands. But even he, the Lord of Deceit, works for the Almighty in secret."

My grandmother had come to this conclusion about God after having lived through much of the tragedy of the twentieth century before she died at the age of ninety-nine. Her father was a lower Russian nobleman from the famous Orloff family. He was a theologian and scholar; he married a German girl whom he met when he had gone to "take the waters" in the spa of Aachen for health reasons. He was attached to the Czarist Embassy in London, where they raised their family. Later he taught Slavic literature at King's College of London University. Their five children—including my grandmother—were torn apart by the First World War's stupidity, by Europe's nationalism, and the little war games played by the ruling families of England, Germany, and Russia. Immediate relatives were caught up in these deadly dramas, fighting on all sides and against each other. One sister disappeared in Russia's Marxist rivalries; one brother arrived just in time to the funeral of another, though they had fought on opposing lines in the civil war.

My German grandfather lived with his Russian/German/English wife and their family in Belgium, where he had a business. During the first war he fought on the side of Germany opposing both England and Russia. Twice they lost all their belongings when, being German nationals, they were evicted from Belgium. They were devastated a third time when their family house in Germany was bombed at the end of the Second World War.

My own interest in Christianity was confronted by my grandmother's questions—charmingly presented, but revealing a wounded life spent in frequent tragedy and unresolved puzzles. How can there be a good God, or any God at all, when staggering absurdities are played out a million times daily in the lives of our generation?

Seeming meaninglessness can be seen across life's spectrum, from the global to the pedestrian. A woman paid for her purchase and stepped out into the road in Brooklyn, where a stray bullet killed her in an instant. What a difference it would have made if she had not had exact change for her purchase or if she had talked a little longer!

The English philosopher Bertrand Russell suggested in his widely read work *Why I Am Not a Christian* (1967) that when we face real life we must conclude that there is no God, or that God is evil, or that God is too weak to do anything about cruelty, death, and pain. There is simply no way to bring "almighty" and "good" together in a descriptive sentence about God. If the deity were good, he could *and would* do something to set the world aright. But he has not. If God is evil and mighty, reality could be explained, but this being should be called the Devil and actively resisted. In the third alternative, God as good but weak, good is without much import; reality could be explained, but there would be no reason to worship this being. By definition he would not be "God," but a weak, wishful and finally, *failed* creator.

It is little wonder that many serious persons in the past century have concluded that reality itself demands a stand against evil, but not on the basis of religion or revelation. Where there is a vacuum of gods or human goodness to effect real change, reason demands an effort to fight—even by means of revolution—as a way to authenticate our humanity against the silent, cruel and deadly world.

In my experience the church has not for the most part addressed these issues with any amount of seriousness. In the name of Christianity, people have advocated a mysterious weakness of God, his victory through an existential embrace of death. We have heard of the *theology of hope*, which says that in spite of all reality, only hope in a better future gives us a goal toward which to believe and dream. We have heard of progress somewhere moved by invisible forces from the depth of the earth or from a deeper understanding of God, a stance which in essence invites further irrationality. Since Kierkegaard in the nineteenth century, such irrationality has been admitted as a source for faith and hope. There is perhaps no finer way to absolve the Church from an obligation to speak the truth. An advocacy of the irrational just does not cut it when we need an explanation of good and evil.

We have heard of *faith in faith*, the merit of believing something as a confession together with others, even though we can't explain it or relate it to evidences in slices of reality. Francis Schaeffer's repeated use of the picture of an upper-story experience for this sort of view is helpful and fitting. With it he illustrates that modern man has abandoned a unified field of knowledge, in which both factual information (what relates to earth, things, time, and nature) and moral/cultural values (which relate to heaven, morals, eternity, and grace) were seen in a coherent manner. The break-up resulted in two separate areas, or stories in a mental building, without a connecting staircase. Man knows factually what mathematics tell him. But morally he has no answer to the question of meaning in any way related to the real world. Man as a person, morals, and meaning are defined according to whim, religion, and wishful thinking. Worse, answers in this realm are found as much through speculation as through a drug trip or any similar existential experience

On the lower story of evidences, facts, and mathematics we conclude that life is real but without meaning or direction and over all quite absurd. No moral evaluation can be made. We are left to measure, count, and weigh, to do research in order to find the quantities of whatever but without any framework for qualitative considerations, for meaning, or ethics in any other way than personal preferences.

"A little bit of religion would be good for you" were Mother's words whenever I fought with my younger brother. But she did not want me to take religion too seriously. Religion should tame teenage anger and frustration but was not expected to give answers from a framework of historically-disclosed truth about the place of humanity in the world. Faith was not meant to inform more than relative cultural morals; it certainly was not meant to offer anything approaching transcendent meaning. Religion could make social machinery run more smoothly, but it should never provide the kind of equipment people and communities need to understand the "What? Whence? Wither?" and to find coherent answers to these questions.

There is an alternative given by much of the Church today to this rather bleak outlook with the suggestion of a subjective benefit to "the true believers" (a term coined by Eric Hoffer). It proposes that God is good and mighty, in control of all things on earth. This deity's sovereignty is unquestioned and celebrated. Any problem from actual life experience brought up against this view is covered by an "umbrella-designation" of humanity's collective and personal sinfulness. First, this attempted explanation goes, we are so terribly sinful that we deserve all we experience. This creates intellectual and cultural dissonance when we see the righteous suffer and perpetuators of evil get away with too much in our lived experience. It is far more obvious that there is really very little justice in the form of deserved punishment for obvious crimes, in the words of Solomon, "under the sun."

Secondly, we are told to believe so strongly in God's sovereignty that all questions or doubts are answered with the "mystery pass" of God's holy and inscrutable counsel. After all, we are told, God in his sovereign holy counsel does all things well, though we cannot understand how this works out in real life. With this notion, God passes out of normal inquiry and becomes inaccessible. Both God's holiness and God's reasons are now matters of blind faith, which our faith posits from fear that God might be otherwise. We only assume that God is holy and reasonable because we are simply too afraid to conclude that he may be evil and irrational.

This "faith" makes quick use of the term "mystery" whenever something does not make intellectual or moral sense. It is a pass, because such a God is beyond the need to show himself innocent of the evil in the real world: He does not respond to this question. But the believer also passes when she has not dared to seek an answer. She can do that with all kinds of excuses for her intellectual laziness or, more passively, when she resolves that it is impossible for humanity to discover comprehensible answers.

Yet this kind of "faith" gets a lot of mileage in Christian circles today. It is more *faith in faith* than acknowledging what makes sense in light of the real world of human beings. This is not, however, what faith as depicted in Scripture demands or honors. In the end it sells biblically-characterized faith short by insisting on certainty about one's own uncertainty! It is the contradictory view that we decide to know for sure what we can not know.

Usually (but not exclusively) this view is connected to John Calvin, though we shall propose it reflects his philosophical descendents more than Geneva's reformer and preacher himself. It is in no way limited to Reformed theology but is the affirming, heart-warming, and confidence-building message in many churches. It has become almost a matter of good manners in theology to affirm that in all life's reality God is in control. Without always knowing the Calvin Connection, this sketch of Calvinism has become the Emily Post of much Christian theology in this question of a broken and unfair world.

We shall see how this can only be believed when passages in the Bible are read out of context to substantiate a system of theology in spite of the Bible's teaching. I will attempt to demonstrate how the Bible is the one text that insists on human personal responsibility, on freedom to create new and even evil situations that are not "willed" by anyone but the creature himself. In contrast to the contemporary discussion, creation itself is an open reality, a stage with many actors. God is not changeable in his character, somehow combining both good and evil. But there *is* an unfinished reality now in the same sense that creation was not finished at the end of six days. I will show how this real openness in all of history is not a result of some finiteness, openness, or indeterminacy on the part of God.

Of course, Scripture teaches that God is both good and mighty. But plucking this isolated truth from the rich tapestry of the Bible as a lone thread could make God the author of any and all events. It would make our understanding of what is good and evil irrelevant. Islam holds such a view. It would answer all the questions relating to meaning, purpose, and power in the human experience in terms of God's will and a necessary blind obedience by human subjects. Nothing would be out of place, no moment unattended by God, no experience out of line, never a real problem. There would be one player in reality, and we would be many pawns within the divine purposes.

This perspective would link God inextricably to our reality, which we experience as good and evil. God reigns over existence in sovereignty. Revelation of God's will and character would not only be found in the prophetic word of the Bible but in all events of history. Both God and creation would describe what is. Nothing would prescribe what should be, for everything already follows a sovereign order. That view goes to the core of questions human beings have forever posed. Without a more differentiated answer, the moral person must conclude that God orchestrates in some intimate and powerful way all that happens, and the assassination of JFK in Dallas is just one small part of the concert of events in history.

If anything remains wrong in history at all, any court of law would be obliged to declare that the evidence establishes the guilt of God.

With this view of sovereignty, questions of morality, human purpose, government, meaning and worship are also disregarded and given no answer. We are but players under the baton of God in his orchestra. We must practice to be rewarded in our lives; we have the professional sensitivity to despise the score but are not allowed to change it.

I find it curious that when more and more among our contemporaries seek to find an anterior cause in the past, someone or something to blame (or to praise) for their life, personality, sexual orientation, and criminal behavior, the Church so often does not give the truly liberating answer of definite individuality, of choice and effort rewarded and of responsibility pronounced. Instead the Church joins the choir of other determinists: God did it all. "It's the Lord's doing." Genetics, psychological scars, and inherited traits are all part of our nature, and "God willed it all," if you believe what you hear in many sermons or personal conversations. The drunken driver is not really responsible for the death of the child: "God in his wisdom ordained it for some higher purpose" is often the best people and pastors will say to comfort the grieving family.

This should be quite bewildering and troubling; this view does not easily square with other indications in the Bible where we see God struggling with a fallen world. God seems to be often outraged, disappointed even, and then intervening from moral disapproval in the course of events. There are the tears of Christ over an unbelieving Jerusalem or when faced with a dead friend Lazarus; Jesus did not accept the arguments of the Pharisees as final. His responses to the needy crowds of the sick, the lame, the confused, and exploited, or to disciples who are "of little faith" contain no reference to some ulterior purpose to their plight. His complaints about "this adulterous generation" asking for signs (Matthew 12:39, 16:4) or being ashamed of him and his words (Mark 8:38) are not softened with declarations of some divine purpose or references to God's permissive will. Adulterers can hardly expect signs of affection from their discarded spouse and should experience guilt when they dismiss the words of their lover. They, like Adam and Eve and all their children before, have walked away from the knowledge of and the relationship with their creator.

Jesus does not, even in a hidden way, approve of the situation or the attitude of the generation to whom he spoke. Such a response serves no educational purpose and has no spiritual benefit. They need to change their thinking and their lives lest they lose their souls. People are at a crossroad before a choice and not on a broad boulevard designed to smoothly lead everyone along.

In these pages we will see that when God is in charge of all that happens, he is no longer the God of the Bible. Scripture is more nuanced than what we are left with after some systematic theologies have attempted to reduce it *systematically*. The biblical account presents us with several players after creation. The persons of the Trinity loved and acted among themselves forever. Humanity is created in God's image. Angels live in their own sphere. Creation is outside of God, for he looked at it and called it good. In the Bible alone, personality has been around forever, while matter or energy is created impersonal, without ideas, creativity, language, love, or abstract imagination.

The eternality of impersonal energy is taught in materialism. But even an eternal God can be practically impersonal, when God—as, for instance, in monism—has no one to love, talk to, or enjoy, for he is eternally alone. If Marxism or naturalism teaches impersonal materialism, Islam as monism illustrates impersonal theism.

When God identifies with all of history, there will be no real moral distance between the acts of God and the acts of humanity. Yet the Bible speaks of a history that is torn open by the fall of Adam and Eve, as well as by Satan's rebellion. There is now a gap between who God is and how humanity behaves. "Be ye holy, even as I am holy" is a command to reduce the gap (see Leviticus 19:2; 1 Peter 1:16). It summarizes a whole series of passages that show how much God does not identify with either individual or social history. With the revelation of the death and resurrection of the Messiah, the power of God is historic and gives rise to hope. But that only makes sense when the revelation of the fall of humanity and its consequences in a broken world clarifies God's innocence and defends his moral character.

I am not a professional theologian and do not enjoy "theologizing." My background is in law and theology, a humble participant of that line of believers who struggle with the light of Scripture in the context of life rather than as a separate discipline. Both Calvin and Luther belong to this large group of lawyer/theologians among God's children who saw in Scripture a way to understand God's instruction about life in a fallen world. Scripture sets out what is good and right to encourage humanity. The Bible declares what is sinful and foolish to redirect our energies toward righteousness, opening good, just, and true possibilities to us in belief and work, love, and sex—in other words, in the full circle of life.

Let others pursue their theological pastime like many play golf or the stock market. I'm not active in *any* of these three arenas either! But it does seem to me that in seeking ever more detailed justifications for carefully-honed positions, many theologians may already have lost the audience that experiences a broken, seemingly absurd reality. Theologians whose calling is to present the word (logos) of God (theos) have many times made it easier to have intellectual and moral reasons to reject *God*. His passion, holiness, and love are but hollow concepts unless God's innocence in the mess of reality is clearly established.

That innocence of God is revealed in Scripture. Other religions attempt to cool your emotions, normalize your troubles, and relate you into a much bigger cycle of normalcy, merging you into an "eternal" perspective where injustice loses its meaning. Judaism and Christianity, by contrast, call you apart: to think, learn, discover, and enjoy what God, the eternal Word, has spoken about the origin of the real mess we are in and how to clean it up. God is at work against the real-life troubles we experience in our daily lives. Why then do we still simply accept them and call on God to justify them?

Before she died, my grandmother had come to see the love, credibility, and promises of the God of the Bible. It is my endeavor to paint this same portrait for you here, in true and vivid colors.

CHAPTER ONE

THE GOD WHO REVEALS
GOD'S SELF

Nature's "Glass Darkly"

For many New Yorkers, a visit to Phillips Manor is perhaps the first introduction to what life on a farm with domesticated animals is like. The Bronx Zoo is a paradox: wildlife surrounded by a subway line, commuter trains, and tall buildings. Further west flows the Hudson, across which the lure of wilderness has for centuries drawn people away from human habitat, civilization, and the city. Nature lay beyond the river, over the mountains of Pennsylvania and Virginia. The Mississippi was the continent's divide before the walls of the Rocky Mountains. The self-made man, hunting, settling, and then moving on again, was closely associated with being in nature in years past, in an era where one could prove one's qualities and avoid the pitfalls of having neighbors.

Fast-forward to decades later. Anyone who did not pioneer for whatever reason can quite easily buy his own house and tend his lawn on his plot, pretending he is taming and experiencing nature. Nature is being close to the ground, master in one's own homestead, one's ear and heart attuned to wilderness, far away from the shouts and cries of the city. There is a harmony not easily found among people. Nature—in all her majesty, silence, and novelty—is romantically perceived as a divine temple.

In no way was this typical of the new world of the Americas. Germans love their forests, glens, and brooks. The Sunday walk has largely replaced attendance at church. Scandinavians love their birch forests, ponds, and moors. French have replaced church with rabbit hunts or local tastes at the nearest café. The English hike over the Downs.

Perhaps humanity is so often in search of nature because it is our closest neighbor, yet one that does not talk back, with its hidden ways and energies. From it we draw our food and drink and to it we return at death to dust. There is movement without too much chaos, change with great regularity of seasons and tides; there are cycles of birth and death, and the sun seemingly goes round and round.

Isaiah Berlin draws an interesting line to connect such an embrace of nature with the eighteenth-century Romantic Movement, where the individual expresses what is on his personal wish list. Religious enthusiasts have similar ideas of freedom from reality. As reaction to society and everything that is of human invention, they express a return to a more pagan view. Even the familiar ideologies of democracy—fascism, Marxism, and secular humanism—assume that a more advanced order for life now proceeds from human nature; a way of life more holistic and relevant than their parents' sources in Christianity and Judaism. The "natural" human being is closer to his real self, where men and women discover their own divinity through imagination and dreams.

In our generation we have perhaps advanced a further step, suggesting that the adjective "human" caused a problem by differentiation from the rest of nature, a threat to all else, and should therefore be made less central. Nature has become the model. Animals are studied to direct our attention to how we should now live. Submission to an ecosystem is now valued more than human distinctives, because the human is seen as the source of all Earth's problems.

The distinction between humanity and the rest of creation as uniquely crafted in the image of God and not part of nature exclusively, is rooted in the biblical affirmation. The mandate to exercise dominion elevates us into places of responsibility, creativity, and change agency. Nonetheless, it violates the notion of a fundamental unity with our surroundings and therefore is seen only as a problem, not also a part of all major solutions.

For more than fifty years David Attenborough has taken us into the world of animals around the world by means of exciting and detailed documentaries about their natural habitats. He observes them from close range, lies in their paths and then describes their lives, feeding, and mating habits in their ecosystems with wonder and fascination. One would expect that with so much sensitive exposure to the animal world and nature he would advocate a reduced role for humankind in greater humility to a nature that perhaps reveals the divine.

During a recent interview on BBC television in appreciation of his life and career, he was asked whether all his experience and research has made him more aware of "someone like, you know, a creator behind these marvels of animal life." His response, after a very brief pause, was the reflection of a very observant scientist. He said something like this: "When I expose people to such marvels, such majesty and details of animal life, I also have in mind at the same time, the horror for that small boy in the Congo region of Africa, whose eye is at that same moment slowly penetrated by a river worm from behind, where his brain is, after it has wormed its way all through the body from his feet upwards. I have to keep both glory and horror in mind. When I do that, I do not see a benign creator in all this."

He continued to say that many people sentimentalize their observation of nature. But for him such an interpretation misses the reality of what he loves to show. These observers see only what they wish to see, such as the glory in primitive natural life always ordered by habit and instinct. Even talk about the food chain reveals a delight in its orderliness but misses the reality of its cruelty.

Woody Allen acknowledges this cruelty in his own observant and realistic way when he speaks of nature as a "giant restaurant." If God wants the lamb and lion to lie down together in such a world, the lamb better keep a very watchful eye on the lion.

Sentimentality about nature's ways is one of the human responses to the many questions reality raises. We can admire something's orderliness, even when it has painful and destructive elements. We call something cute or majestic, cuddly or wild, because we wish to see it as such. We would feel very differently if we either looked more closely or had to live in the midst of the untamed wild for all our life; if instead of domesticating animals, we were now told to live like what many call "the animal within us."

Attenborough's camera does not go through intellectual reflection. It does not compare and contrast. It responds to the way it is held and takes pictures according the producer's actions on its mechanism. It feels no distance between what shows up in the lens and what ought to be there. Attenborough himself, however, makes a moral judgment about the camera's observation and then draws a philosophical conclusion from it. He notices the conflict between beauty and horror: even though the worm only functions in accordance with its circumstances and instincts, Attenborough transcends the moment and sees in his mind what will happen to the boy. He compares this with what he wishes the boy to experience instead. And he can imagine what it would feel like if the worm were crawling into his own eye.

There is very little room for sentimentality in observing nature. One must admire the workings of nature and bring them closer to the casual observer and ignorant city dweller. One may be tempted to grant room for nature to follow its way without demanding its compliance with our standards of moral selection. At the moment where such ways intersect and influence our human existence, however, or even threaten the survival of other animal species we start viewing nature through our moral lenses. While nature functions on instinct and in accordance with nature's laws, we also notice that it prevents no threat to survival and respects no rights or dignities. Humanity requires a moral law above the natural law, for we value human life and assert a sense of what the Bible gives as the mandate to human beings: to subdue the earth and to have dominion, to multiply and to work with our hands and minds against thorns and thistles so that another generation can continue when our own bodies return to the dust from which they were taken.

Sentimentality is one unacceptable response to nature's ways. Careful observation, reflection, and moral responses are required in a world of precise definitions. When we recognize that we do not live in a harmonious ecosystem but instead in one where big eats little and little can destroy big, we require tools of discernment, skills for survival, and moral direction in order for life to have continuity and death in its many manifestations to be restrained.

Another unacceptable response is to create a category called "mystery." We place all the things we do not (now or presumably ever) understand into the "mystery" box. There are mysteries of course, occurring when we experience events or observe slices of reality which we assume belong together but cannot connect at present. For instance, how does the body know the exact time when labor starts the birth of a child. What directs migrating birds to find their way to their destination and back? How about salmon returning to their sweet water spawning grounds after having grown to adulthood in the salty ocean? Why did Lisa ever choose to marry Tom (*Any resemblance to persons living or dead purely coincidental*) in light of what even we know about each of them?

Among human beings it always puzzles me why we make the choices we make. Even if I know my own reasoning, I certainly don't understand some of the choices others make. My wife, Deborah, and each of my five children still are a mystery to me in many ways. They are outside me, well-known strangers. They love and are reliable, trustworthy, and always there, but who are they . . . really? I do not know with any finality for I am finite, in many ways a mystery to myself.

Yet we must be careful to separate these mysteries, in which we gain insight gradually through experience and science, from what is quite casually called "mystery" in the frequently suggested relationship between God and nature, or God and history. All too readily people wish to see God in nature, so the question was put to David Attenborough. I held my breath while listening and was so relieved to hear that with all his observations about animal life he could not see a benevolent God in nature in spite of all the majesty he observed there over the years. For, nature's majesty also bears the face of cruelty; all the strength of life also gives off whiffs of death. All the orderliness loses its shine in instinctual-but-violent attacks and the loss of life in the giant food chain and lust for blood.

Perhaps we should tread carefully before sending postcards and hanging posters presenting Bible verses on a background of autumn foliage, mountain scenes, and immaculate beaches. A closer look at these picturesque scenes would give a far more mixed insight. We would quickly realize the presence of death as well. If God's character is revealed more in nature than in the world of human beings made in his image, we have either God's moral character hidden in mystery, or sentimentalized cruelty.

The God Who is Near

Among human beings—in their art and efforts, their unpredictable choices to love, speak, and create; in their concerns about pain or about peace in the midst of society's imperfections—we more readily find something of the Bible's addresses to people. And in people we see what the Bible reveals of God's being. We are *his* children, not the children of nature. We are not fully at home in nature; we more readily abide in what God said about taking dominion and building family, relationships, and homes against the surrounding wilderness.

The God of the Bible is not obscured in mystery, nor are his intentions mysterious. He has said things and shown things. His acts are revealed and described so that we would understand them (Deuteronomy 29:29). His speaking addresses our minds and needs to be understood, otherwise it is only a cacophony of syllables. Understanding the text, the sentences, the paragraphs, and the flow of Scripture's argument requires considerable effort. This should not surprise us. Any piece of literature, contract, or love letter also requires such effort. What do the words mean? Where else is this subject treated? What could it not possibly mean? How can I discover whether it is meant honestly? Where is there evidence to support the assertions? What can I do to complain if the words are not honored?

The God of the Bible is not *totaliter aliter* or wholly other. His word is not indirect, full of hidden meanings and reversed values. Of course there are depths to God's being that we do not fathom. We were not present at creation. We have now been evicted from the garden and depend on letters from God to inform us until a time when he will again dwell among us and we with him. He has sent his Spirit so that the spiritual death and alienation we experience as orphans, ignorant and with little comfort here now, is removed and spiritual life becomes a reality.

The concept of a *totally other* God comes from philosophy, not from the Bible or history, though many theologians have embraced it to justify their acceptance of the irrational as a source of knowledge. This delight in the irrational extends to many impossible explanations of Christ's death and resurrection, which has plagued modern theology since the nineteenth century. It is built on the assumption that for God to be God he would have to be totally different from us. Since we think in terms of time (finiteness), reason (words and syntax), and causation (science, analysis, and deductions), God must be timeless (infinite), irrational (feeling, spiritual) and full of unexpected surprises compared to our standards and ways of thinking and doing.

The problem is that this conclusion forgets that the God of the Bible made us in his image and able to understand God's communications, though not exhaustively. This God has created a real universe where he is not a stranger. He talked with Adam and Eve, came for lunch with Abraham, and in other multiple occasions talked, explained, and demonstrated his sovereignty over Pharisees. Further, he pronounced his judgment of bad blood between people, expressed his revulsion over sickness, and openly asserted his authority over evil spirits and finally death itself.

In fact Jesus says, to the surprised and opposing Pharisees in John 10:33–38, that the judges over Israel (who are called *elohim*, a name normally reserved for God, in the Psalm Jesus quotes, 82:6!) could understand God's word to instruct them in how to make just choices in their obligations to serve the people. The Bible speaks of an infinite God, who is not timeless in some sort of "eternal now," but eternal in sequences of "before" and "after" relationships. Time unfolds like a sequence in the relationship between the persons of the Trinity before creation. From God's perspective, we are now living in a time after the fall. In the same way God's relation to people is different *before* the birth of Christ "in the fullness of time" and *after* his glorification. Different aspects of God himself are disclosed at various times. These are not merely what *seem* to be sequences from our finite human perspective.

God is an infinite person with clear and consistent characteristics, whose depth we cannot ever reach or absorb, but whose personality is evident, accessible, and trustworthy. With God things and events are the way they appear to us to be, when his actions and the verbal explanations of his actions are carefully observed and understood. God exhaustively knows all things and events. From God we receive a reliable witness to things and events with enough of a verifiable context to allow us to know them truthfully. Reality, including the reality of God's being and character, is never just an illusion or something "totally other," either in creation or in the finished work of Christ.

Of course, there is always "something more" we can discover about God. This is not surprising, since "something more" can always be said and discovered about all reality as well. No object, person, or situation is ever completely known by us in our finiteness. Inexhaustible knowledge is the continuing challenge and privilege for any finite being. But the "inexhaustible," by definition, touches on the quantity of knowledge, not its quality. It does not mean that limited knowledge is necessarily erroneous. True knowledge about God—though finite—does not imply that what we know of God is in the end contrary to what God has said and done.

Francis Schaeffer speaks of the infinite-personal and personal-infinite God in his lectures and books. Our visit to a German university showed us the importance of this qualified infinity and eternal character of God. The materialists in the audience needed to hear about the person of God, and the pietists in the audience needed the clarification of God's infinite character.

Mystery According to Scripture

There are essentially three areas in which the Bible speaks of mystery. Daniel was able to know the king's dream and explain its meaning. God revealed it to him to show that he, Daniel, knew things from God, unlike the king's diviners who played guessing games. This mystery relates to how God can make something known about future events.

Paul speaks of the mystery of our resurrection, a sure event that will become evident. This mystery surprises by its powerful abolition of death at the hand of the creator for whom the death of persons is not the end.

The central mystery referred to in Scripture relates to the way of salvation: Can humanity's fall or my own failures ever be undone when time has moved on from the events? How is it possible? Is there any hope to recover fellowship with God, moral restitution, and peace of mind? Who would accomplish it, and when would we be certain of it? This mystery deals with what God is able to interpose to remove guilt without becoming guilty himself.

The promise in Genesis, in the immediate context of Adam's fall and a creation spoiled by the effects of sin, speaks of God doing what amounts to an additional work. A moral or legal dilemma now existed through our first parents' choice to turn their back on God and believe a lie. A second dilemma arose when physical death eventually followed the moral death from sin.

God's additional work consisted first of running after Adam and Eve to promise restoration. This would redress the legal dilemma of personal guilt by a work of God, who—in the second person of the eternal Trinity, God the Son—would receive a body from a woman and crush Satan's head for good (Genesis 3:15). The Lord and judge of the universe would take the result of our sin, true moral guilt, on himself. He as judge, rather than we as the guilty party, would suffer and bear the consequences to pay for the wrong. He would absorb divine alienation so that we would become God's children again.

The repeated sacrifices of lambs without blemish in the Old Testament liturgy dramatized this entire transaction: sin, guilt, and their lethal consequences are unavoidable until God, through the infinite moral value of his son's death, accomplished the legal and factual reality of forgiveness once for all. This is real history. There is a time and space component to it. From the "My God, my God, why have you forsaken me," to the "It is finished" on the cross, the judgment was enacted.

God also instructs Adam and Eve at the time of the Fall, and repeats it through the prophetic teaching and the law in increasing detail to later generations: humanity must work together in a sweaty effort against death and fragmentation to live in the expectation of their Savior. The legal problem would be healed when the eternal judge of the moral universe would take our punishment on himself. He would deal with the factual problems that resulted from sin by the power of his resurrection, a first-fruit of a larger and richer harvest. In addition he would deal with the problem of ignorance, confusion, and social tension by means of the Law. Its application would diminish the legal, moral, and personal chaos of people surrounded by a reality of hideous contradictions in natural and unanswered questions about truth, reality, right, and wrong.

The central mystery Scripture speaks of concerns the *how* and *when* of the fulfillment of this promise, which is clearly stated and repeatedly confirmed through the whole Bible. The rest of the mystery of the promise is explained in enough detail to leave no room for confusion. The question of whether God had caused suffering and injustice would be clearly addressed, demonstrating that sin and the resulting evil were creations of the creature, not of God. God had no hand in them. Adam and Eve created a new situation by their choice to question God's truth. They stupidly believed in the serpent's impossible promise that they, created beings, would be like the eternal God.

In Greek religions, "mysteries" described secret rites into which people were solemnly initiated. The word implies a select insight purposefully hidden from others to express exclusivity. The Gnostic philosophers spoke frequently of mysteries, private insights about the divine way to escape the prison of the material world, including the human body. The Church went to great effort to distance the insight of the Bible from such a focus on personal directives, mysterious knowledge, and "other" goals. Jesus does not exist in the heart of people, in their inner conviction, or in their emotions. He existed for us first on earth ("For in Christ all the fullness of the Deity lives in bodily form" Colossians 2:9) and then after the resurrection and ascension on the right hand of the Father in heaven ("Jesus Christ . . . has blessed us in the heavenly realms with every spiritual blessing in Christ" Ephesians 1:3).

In stark contrast to mystery religion, the Bible does not know secret rites. All things are out in the open. All ritual is explained and given a broader historic and intellectual context. The word of God is given to declare truth and reality to the whole world. The mind is addressed and sharpened by it to make any confusion with imagined gods and lifestyles obviously foolish.

In the Bible "mystery" refers to details not yet known, things which will be revealed later in order to complete what is now known in part. Salvation contains no mystery about *what* God will do, but about *how* and *when*. Mystery does not relate to God's attitude towards people or his actions on their behalf. The mystery component concerns the question of how it will all work out eventually before human eyes.

The book of Job in the Old Testament sheds much light on the fundamental questions about God's absence, his justice, the kind of world we live in, and what can be done about it. In Job we find encouragement to ask difficult questions. They are in many ways the core of why our contemporaries reject Christianity in favor of religions, with all the damage they cause in soul, spirit, and culture. Job and his story shall form the touchstone for much of our conversation on the character of God in these pages.

Job is rewarded for his refusal to accept his friends' advice. They are wrong to believe that our lives are fair now. Job's experiences are tragic. He suffers the consequences of a heavenly battle through no fault of his own. He has done no wrong to deserve what he experiences. He demands that God show himself and explain the unfairness of all his suffering and loss of family. And God does. It is important to realize that God is no contemporary Christian in his response! Job is told neither to accept a mystery, nor that because he is a sinner he deserves death and should be glad that he at least is still alive when his children are already dead.

Instead, Job is honored in several ways. God does eventually show up; he judges Job's friends in their foolishly simplistic assumptions about reality being fair. Is it not true that "under the sun" (as Solomon describes the span of our birth and death in Ecclesiastes) "all is vanity?" There is no resolution now, no justice unless it includes what follows after death: the balancing of the books and the resurrection.

God also points out to Job that reality is more complex than meets the eye. As "omniscient readers" of Job we know why: we have the book's prelude, in which the accusation and challenge from Satan against Job and any believer is disclosed. A curtain is opened on a second "stage" above that of visible history disclosing a war for a while between God and the rebellious and accusing angel who wanted to be like God. This fallen angel is the accuser of the brethren who seeks to devour some. But there is no mystery about what God will do. Job was right to have that confidence. His knowledge was only limited to the when and how, which God points out by reminding Job that this heavenly battle is very serious and of long duration. Reality has become extremely complex ever since the fall of both angels and humanity affected all creation, but that does not make it at all confusing to God.

First Corinthians 15:51 talks about the "mystery" that we shall not all sleep, but we shall all be changed at the coming of Christ. In 1 Corinthians 2:1 Paul says that he did not come to Corinth with eloquent speech or what the Greeks understood to be wisdom when he proclaimed the mystery of God. Here Paul distinguishes

God's available knowledge from that of Greek mystery religions. The latter was open to a select few who passed the muster of philosophers whose authority rested on their fine speech, high ideals, and contemplation of beauty. The former is revealed to everyone, for God's Spirit knows the mind of God and has revealed it to us (1 Corinthians 2:6ff).

The "mystery of faith" mentioned in 1 Timothy 3:9 refers to precisely the details of what we believe for good reasons, affirmations which should be held confidently by elders of the church. They should not hide this mystery but be apt to teach it because they are convinced of it after critical discernment. Otherwise, why would honest people teach it in good conscience?

Ephesians addresses the desire to declare the mystery of the gospel with boldness (6:19). Paul speaks of the mystery of Christ having been revealed (3:3–4), so that he and the recipients of his letter could understand it. In the first chapter he speaks of the fact that the mystery of God's will has been made known in Christ's coming, work, and purpose (v. 9). In Christ, he says, we have every spiritual blessing already in heavenly places (v. 3). In Christ we are chosen (v. 4) and adopted (v. 5). In and through him God has lavished his grace on us (v. 6). In Christ we have redemption and forgiveness (v. 7). This is the "mystery" now made known to Jew and Gentile in the fullness of time, when God summed up all things in Christ (v. 10).

Colossians, a letter to a church that was very much exposed to Gnostic mystery ideas, has Paul again explain that the mystery is related to the person of Christ. He asks God "to fill [the people] with the knowledge of his will through all spiritual wisdom and understanding" so that they may please God in every way, bearing fruit in every good work. The first two chapters are dedicated to the reality that whatever mystery there is has now been made manifest in public, "disclosed to the saints" (1:26).

This is the tenor of Scripture's treatment of "mystery." Peter speaks of it in terms of the prophets before Christ seeking and searching the promised salvation diligently, when they prophesied of the grace that would come to Peter's audience and those who would read his letter in generations to come: "Concerning this salvation, the prophets, who spoke of the grace that was to come to you, searched intently and with the greatest care, trying to find out the time and circumstances to which the Spirit of Christ in them was pointing when he predicted the sufferings of Christ and the glories that would follow." (1 Peter 1:10–11).

Mystery, then, is not what some people think in secret, even though they cannot know, think, or understand it. Neither does it relate to something about a far-off place, cut off from material reality, the mind, or moral and intellectual categories. According to the Bible, mystery is something quite specific of which fuller understanding is a matter of time, not relegated to feeling or make-believe. We shall see in Scripture that the reason why a person believes in God or his Christ is not a mystery. There is no mystery either, nor mere subjectivity in the soul of a person, about God's word and work. Knowing God has something to do with a decision to recognize and acknowledge the Lordship of the Creator, the redeemer and restorer God.

Many today seem to like their mysteries, much in the same way people in the past liked to see God behind all events. Like constantly changing fad diets and guidelines for eating, mysteries sound very much like neighbors of common gossip and conspiracy theories. Many instances of personal guidance, private readings of Scripture, and spiritual gift inventories reveal a pleasure in personal mysteries and meanings. The reference to "God" in relation to mystery seems useful and pious, but it does not compass a genuine desire to know and realize. Instead it fosters a persistent ignorance of what is factual, coherent, and true in light of how God's word relates to the evidence of life.

Nature Remains Silent

An appeal to "mystery" also opens the door for suggesting that the natural world is always tied to some hidden moral purpose through God's immediate intervention. In this paradigm, natural disasters, illness, and unjust governments are all attributed to the hand of God. Some take Scripture's affirmation that God sustains all things by the word of his power (see Hebrews 1:3) to mean that no apple falls off the tree until God withholds his word to keep it there. They seek a reasonable and powerful explanation behind all events and thus credit God as the mover behind all events. Greeks and other pagan societies see such an "animus" or mind behind all natural events. This animistic belief at times refers to a moral will and other times the mere power behind events. Through this perception events like personal injuries or fortunes could be explained, as well as natural phenomena, such as an earthquake or a river coming from a source in the side of a hill. Thunder was but the gods bowling, illness the working of an evil spell or a moody deity. "Let the water run, it wants to live in Mombassa," says the African foreman in the film version of *Out of Africa* when the dam is too low to retain the flood. Such an articulation is widely held in many cultures; to me, this is understandable. Nonetheless, I think there are two flaws in this way of thinking and speaking.

First, it fails to see that the "powerful word" referred to in the Bible is the "God spoke and it was" of creation, by which apple trees were made to produce only apples each year, not monkeys or marshmallows. God designed and defined it this way. This is what Christians mean when they say that God ordains everything that comes to pass. His is a coherent and rational universe where cause and effect function and are not subject to odd turns and freak or random events. We shall see that this even relates to the grace of God, which is not a matter of seemingly arbitrary choices.

Second, to see God behind all events seems to do justice to God's power, but it violates God's moral character each time.

When God is behind all things he is not only the *deus ex machina*, but also the reason and source of both good and evil, making him either wicked or incomprehensible. In such a world, the values of "good" and "evil" have lost their real distinctiveness. Reality is then, as in Hinduism, an illusion. Events only seem to be good or evil. In reality they are blank.

The *deus ex machina* of the past was gradually replaced by greater insight and scientific discoveries, fueling mandates to diminish pain, evil, and suffering. These were not expressions of unbelief but of affirmation that we live in an ordered (or "lawful") universe. Such encouragement to discover applicable insights for human life is found only in the Jewish and Christian cultural traditions. It laid the intellectual foundation for that kind of consistent and steady inquiry. The Bible encouraged people to believe that God had made a real universe "upheld by the word of his power." Jews and Christians became culturally innovative, unlike fatalistic Muslims, or Buddhists in perpetual search of detachment. Those standing in the Judeo-Christian lineage are not materialists with the concurrent denial of real significance. Neither are they like African animists, always afraid to unbalance the occult workings of hidden spirits in all parts of nature.

With all our involvement with nature and the discoveries of how it worked, Jews and Christians did not believe that God was acting in all events of a tragic, painful, and problematic world and its history. They did not function from a perspective of inevitable fate or an all-pervasive fairness, or of a puppeteer God. When they acted or interfered with what normally happens in the real world, they were not rebelling against God's plan for the world. They acted in reality, as God himself also does, to flesh out the words of the Lord's Prayer: "Thy will be done on earth (where it is not fully accomplished yet), as it is already being done in heaven." They understood the moral mandate as well and sought to create a better order than what nature, including human nature, provided after the Fall. Adam was told to work against thorns and thistles, to have babies, to love his wife and to improve on what had become a fallen world. Believers saw themselves in that line of thought, judging the world of reality from the standards of the Word about reality, that Word which was before the beginning and then took on flesh to dwell amongst us.

The moral silence of nature was overcome with the language of purpose, life, and a hope well explained in Scripture. Nature, including human nature, was to be transformed into a holy culture. It is anchored in the realization that the eternal Word, who is God and was with God, came into the world and dwelled among us (John 1:1). Our culture is built on this Word, while religion finally maintains a moral indifference. Buddhism and her children teach that silence is a more fitting description of reality. Islam and Marxism use many words and speak, like propaganda, of divine or scientific rules for the world. Yet both produce in effect a silence through words merely repeated collectively and by rote without comprehension and real meaning, without heart and soul.

Our generation fails in our task to carry on the banner of our biblical heritage whenever we appeal to "mystery" where things are in fact explained. We also fail when we succumb to the notion that God's sovereignty is a form of control that leaves people hanging at the end of the wires of a master puppeteer. There is something blind and immoral when responsibility is given to and required from a puppet whose life a sovereign puppeteer controls. This is not a case of "mystery," but of immorality.

Our interest in this whole question is not a matter of friendly discussions among the retired idle. Holding onto the *deus ex machina* suggestion, that whatever has no other explanation must be from God, exposed a nakedness concerning facts of many nineteenth century Christians. Their faith served them very poorly. Science in the form of a more careful study and observation—not faith—improved our hygiene, productivity, and life expectancy.

Similarly, "you will achieve what you believe" is a modern motivational marketing slogan. By itself it does not accomplish anything, and if you act upon it you may well neglect the good and create evil. Faith does not create a new reality any more than belief in a flat earth makes it flat. Situations in the real world require effort, creativity, a choice of priorities and skill in the context of moral evaluation. Scripture does not inform any faith that does not interact with the real world.

Christianity has exposed an intellectual nakedness by believing something the Bible does not teach: all reality is a manifestation of God's character, and the hand of God can be seen in all events. As we will see by contrast, the Bible informs us of a break between the mind of God and the ongoing reality of our experiences. Faith in an *ex machina* God does not overcome real evil, but denies its existence in what is believed to be "God's world." Many Christians believe in their faith but do not really believe the God who speaks in the Bible about the fragility of life in a broken creation.

After the tumultuous events of the twentieth century and the beginning of the twenty-first, Christians are again foolish when they conclude that God was not only present during its inhumanities, but in charge of them. A God who ordains the cruelty of what one neighbor does to another in the name of progressively-intended ideologies must be fought or buried. God cannot be an accomplice to the ends-justify-the-means creeds and manifestos of men. When God's sovereignty is indentured to justify all reality, we cannot possibly place history into the seat of the accused. In this kind of world, Nietzsche and his offspring are the only moral folks left. They will go down as well but with their flag flying.

The God Who is Good

Much of Christianity's contemporary rejection is grounded on these two unbiblical and therefore rather foolish and unnecessary stands: the first is a make-believe faith that is never put on the examining table where creation and history are dissected with the tools provided by Scripture. The second is a failure to acknowledge God's declared war against evil through his acts into and against human history.

Bertrand Russell's objections to Christian faith never dealt with all the jewels of the Bible's teaching. He picked and chose what he wanted to deal with, perhaps all his church ever gave him to think about. His understanding of Christianity was truncated but is what Christians often say and seem to be satisfied with. His response to that kind of Christianity is more honest than that of many Christians.

But there are more jewels in the crown of the biblical God and King. If the first jewel is the existence of a good and almighty God, the second is the information of a historic break with goodness through the fall of Adam and Eve.

The record of this tragic break is of central importance and a distinguishing mark of the Bible, found nowhere else in philosophy or religion. There is a distance between *what was* at creation and for some time afterwards, and *what is* reality as we've known it ever since humanity's fall. God is good and almighty and not the author of evil. His sovereignty is not a control or approval of all events. Only with these two jewels does the third, the work of Christ, become the glorious one in a long row of others. Without the first two we know nothing about a moral and good God. Without the historic fall there is no good God; without God being good, there is no moral compass whatsoever.

Many Christians readily speak of their personal relationship with the Savior, Jesus Christ. They read the New Testament with reverence and the Old with eyes searching for prophesies of salvation to heaven and social programs for earth. But this type of reading does not honestly deal with the text, for the text starts with God, then a good creation, then a real fall by choice, before it ever gets to the rest. And in those opening chapters the stage is set for all that follows with its tragic choices and gracious battles for the crown of God's creation: humankind, male and female in the image of God.

But if God planned it all and sovereignly executed what took place at the Fall, God would need a savior or we would only be victims of his moves. What does it matter whether I have a personal relationship with Jesus if it remains unsettled whether God is at fault? Who would want to spend an eternity with a God whose sovereign plan was to orchestrate a monstrous history?

CHAPTER TWO

A JUST GOD IN AN UNJUST WORLD

The Surprise of a Just God

One of the pleasures of visiting Europe is the exposure to history. People have lived here and left their marks all over the place. They believed that reality needs order, forests need light, and life needs greater protection against death. When they did die, they left their graves marked, their poetry in the hands of another generation, and their paintings on the walls of caves and then museums. They passed knowledge to others in texts, buildings, laws, and landscapes, for they understood themselves to be more than a wave of humanity or part of the natural ebb and flow of things. They built roads and cities, harbors and places of reflection and religion.

They did not see themselves as insignificant, ready to be forgotten or to merge with the environment. They settled rather than be pushed by circumstances. They built with stone against wind and weather, rather than allowing their traces to be blown away as in a nomadic culture. They left their imprint on the face of the earth. After human and natural catastrophes they started again with what they had learned from mistakes.

I like to take our students to Geneva to show them some of that history. Fabius Maximus in 112 B.C. conquered the Allobroges where later Julius Caesar would do the same with the Helvetians in the narrow Rhone valley that slices through the Jura range of mountains. Today it is better known as the place where John Calvin preached the Reformation in the sixteenth century, after another French jurist, William Farel, had told him that it was God's will for Calvin to take over. Henri Dunant founded the Red Cross there in the nineteenth century. In that tradition the League of Nations there debated weakly about a safer world. Now various UN organizations continue to enjoy Geneva.

Among other places of interest, we go to the Cathedral of St. Pierre, where Calvin, the sixteenth-century theologian and minister, preached three times each Sunday and once every other day for the people of the town to hear the good news of God's grace in Christ Jesus. John Knox, father of Scottish and later American Presbyterianism, studied and preached there for a couple of years. Dutch, Hungarians, Germans, and others came to learn what eventually produced an amazing culture of faith, reason, and action. Calvin's teaching and writing, together with that of a multitude of other reformers, brought back to people something much more biblical, humane, and accessible than they had had for generations.

It is worth noting that from our present perspective we would not see as "humane" the way people were constrained by law under threat of punishment to hear this word. The pursuit of a public order often went too far. (Even today Australians are punishable by fines if they do not vote in elections.) But then the times were often chaotic, and citizens of Geneva enjoyed other freedoms. Humane favor *could* be seen in teaching from the Bible about God caring for, loving, and seeking the human being to instruct him about the fuller circumference of life and the certainty of salvation offered in Christ.

People in the pew heard of the love of God, of a purposeful human existence on earth, and of a free and gracious salvation that God has worked for us in Jesus Christ. Farel used the Bible as a textbook in schools around Aigle and later in Neuchâtel in Switzerland. It would become, in its translations into the vernacular, a textbook for all of life. In the Bible, people found a set of glasses that allowed them to see reality in its accurate form, its real dimensions, to help them stumble about less than with the glasses of paganism. With biblical glasses they were also able to distinguish the tragic components that needed to be diminished through skill, dedication, responsibility, and effort across all human disciplines.

Freedom from Fatalism

The teaching and narrative from the Bible relieved people from the pervasive fatalism that is assumed anywhere the God of the Bible is not known. Religions pass on what amounts to a way to get lost, to enter the water without causing a ripple, thereby diminishing the experience of pain. We should just fit into the flow of the way things are! By contrast, the Bible tells us to stand up, think and discover what our responsibilities are in the continuing war against resignation and indifference.

Fatalism is not only the belief in fates behind the appearances of things. In a more general sense I use "fatalism" to describe the belief that our lives are controlled by something prior and outside. Our actions are determined and are in fact reactions. We are not ever creators of a new reality. Reactions do not need to be determined by someone specific. The impersonal universe can also be seen as a mighty mechanism where energy shoves energy and nothing original or new ever happens. All religions I am familiar with—whether transcendent or materialistic—teach such a fatalistic approach. We are to merge with something bigger than ourselves, more powerful and eternal, mostly hidden, yet seen to dictate whatever comes to pass. Freedom, responsibility, and creativity are illusory. Each of us has a destiny that will inevitably happen to us.

The repeated phrase in Didérot's *Jacques Le Fatalist* is "C'est écrit en haut." In Soviet Russia's materialism, the energy of the stars and the forces of history determined the reality of an individual's marriage, health, and death. Your fate or destiny is determined, the outcome already fixed. In reincarnation your present life determines the next in the same way in which your present is also the outworking of all previous lives. In East Asian religions the individual merges with the One, with the state of pure Being. The human being is but a leaf on the river of time. A Zen Koan says, "Man enters the water and causes no ripple." In traditional African religions, you accept and participate in the delicately balanced occult wheel of life and death. In modern Western culture, your genes determine your personality.

This pervasive perspective has its advantages. Nothing is ever out of place; all events fit into a seamless cloth, be it "history," "the will of God," or "scientific inevitability." Whether this fate is personal (as in Islam) or impersonal (as in materialism), formed by geography or by weather makes no difference. The total control of a closed system is common to all these views. Also common is the dreadful consequence that you have died as a real person. There is no "self," no "I" or "me" of personhood. I understand that Japanese children are raised to learn a language that avoids personal pronouns.

Buddhism is often held up as a peaceful religion, especially where people in the more Christian cultures have grown tired of moral obligations to interfere against evil and for good. The choice then is either to labor over what is good and just or to abandon that responsibility outright. Buddhism is a religion leading to indifference, not peace. It teaches individual spiritual detachment and discoveries on the path towards enlightenment that care little about a broken, suffering world. It avoids discovery of conflicts and teaches detachment from moral categories as a way of denial. It is a very selfish pursuit, as can already be seen in Prince Siddharta's own escape from the obligation towards his wife, his baby and the old man dying under the tree. There Buddha finds his enlightenment and consequently does . . . nothing at all.

As a result of the Bible's teaching, we sign our paintings and poems, we give our name to inventions like *Diesel* or *Mercedes Benz* and *pasteurization*. We not only inherit history, we also create it. It started with Adam and Eve creating their particular relationship and having their children because God told them to do that. God did not create it for them. He gave them the form and the mandate. But the reality of love, trust, sex, language, and creation was theirs. They, not God, gave names to the animals. They were to take dominion over creation, to subdue it, and to work in it. History would never be the same as each person, each generation, would build or destroy, be alert or asleep in their significant choices. This is far more than, but in character with, our decision to vote or not vote: either way we make history.

Cultural change through an individual's intellectual and moral change is not an exaggerated description of what the return to God's authority produced. The Protestant Reformation was not a turning to private views or new mysteries; it was a shift from fatalism to significance, from the authority of men to that of God, from superstition and fear to confidence and purpose, from a meaningless puzzle to a fuller picture.

A Fair God

In our modern times John Calvin is most often associated with Calvinism, a particular view of God's relationship with humanity. Calvin shared with other Protestant reformers before and after him the need to inform people again of God's grace and efforts to talk, redeem, clarify, and encourage. Calvin addressed God's pursuit of humanity from his running after Adam to sending the Holy Spirit.

This grace has a specific content; it is not just a good feeling we believe God has about us. Grace is the favor that God has shown us in sending his Son, the second person of the Trinity, to take our place in the judgment we deserve because of our own moral guilt.

Just like Adam and Eve, we have each knowingly done what we understand to be wrong. We are guilty by our wrong choices in a world where our past choices created consequences that we are unable to undo or correct due to the inevitable march of linear history. What has been done remains forever. A broken vase cannot be made new. Adultery cannot be undone. A sharp word stands forever, though others can water down its effect. An apology adds regret to a situation and creates something new but does not remove the consequences of the former injurious choice.

Interestingly, and to show God's total fairness in justice, each person is guilty on the basis of breaking standards he was familiar with and by which he bound the conscience of others (See Romans 2:1–5). For the Jew and Christian that is the standard of the Bible. For the Greek or Roman of Paul's time as much as for everyone in our own generation, guilt is established when a person contradicts in action his own standards of value, however relativistic they may be. Paul addresses this when he establishes guilt for everyone before God in Romans 2. A relativist can only remain true to his view and values as long as he never complains about anyone else's behavior. Any complaint supposes a known and common rule, not a relativistic one. I have never met such a person.

In addition, we have been born into a cracked or broken world that is covered with the dust of death in all places from Adam and Eve on. "Death came to all men," Paul says in Romans 5:12. That is our normal state. Clearly death occurred because of the sin of Adam and Eve and affected all that surrounded and followed them. Everything—humans, nature and the animals, the whole cosmos— is marked by death now, broken and less than the good world God created in the beginning.

But this does not imply that all these parties are guilty. In any court of law, guilt is a matter of choice, not inheritance. Human beings are not morally guilty in some form or other from conception on. The Bible clearly states that we are not guilty for existing, nor is guilt attributed or imputed to us from our parents. We suffer the consequences of their choices but are not blamed for them.

We are innocent in regard to moral guilt, but not innocent in the sense of being pure, simple, or perfect. As children in Adam's race we are no longer free from real brokenness and imperfection. But then, neither are animals or nature free from flaws in the wake of humanity's fall. The whole thing needs a repair job. Humankind needs a repair job for its inherited flaws as well as for its individual moral guilt. We need new bodies without death. Nature needs its cracks and tensions removed to become harmonious without the reality of fright, which is at present part of nature and observable in its food chain.

The repair job is what the good news of Christ's finished work in real history provides. Whether we are initially merely inheritors of imperfections due to the sin of our parents or have ourselves become guilty by continuing their messy ways, God must provide that payment of death, which all imperfection requires. "For the wages of sin is death," (Romans 6:23) and this death was passed to all of us. It is too late for us to repair ourselves. We are already damaged. If you keep the whole law and yet offend in one point you are guilty of it all (James 2:10), for the simple reason that nothing with even a small crack is in any way whole.

Death has passed to all creation, so that the lamb and the lion cannot at this time lie down together. That will have to wait for another day after the change that God will powerfully effect when Christ returns and the last enemy, death, is fully abolished.

There are of course other propositions as to how the brokenness of humanity and nature are to be understood. But I have never been able to follow the so-called Federalist argument. It holds that

Adam represented me in such a way that his guilt stands in a representative way for what would have been my guilt. For, Federalists say, had I been in Adam's situation I would have done the same thing. Well, I can't know that, for I cannot judge backwards into a hypothetical situation from the vantage point of my own present brokenness. Maybe I would have—probably so—but I cannot know that.

Neither is it possible to follow the argument that all reality unrolls under the effects of causation. Things always have an efficient or adequate cause. But human choices often happen for no other prior reason, or weight of influence than that humankind is creative, made in the image of the Creator God. He or she will in part act spontaneously, both within the boundaries of the existing possibilities and also in the frontiers of imagination. The principle of causality does not apply to all reality. It is limited by the ability of persons as moral agents to come up with or to invent ideas, to be self-determining and to *originate* causes.

This does not transfer Heisenberg's Indeterminacy Principle to all reality. But it does suggest that people are a surprise and often create situations that have no prior cause. "Why did you do this?" receives as answer, "Because I wanted to do it." There is a kind of dependent sovereignty or self-determination in each person within a given limiting context such as time and space, gender and personality. That is what God did when he told Adam to have dominion and to love.

Neither is the suggestion that the human being is only the instrumental cause, but not the efficient cause, of events agreeable to Scripture's view of human significance. Consider this illustration. A system of pipes is instrumental for the delivery of water to a fountain. Pipes merely serve someone else's design as means to an end and have no say in the matter. Man is not a mechanism, like a system of pipes, for divine accomplishments. When evil can only be explained as efficiently caused by God, he becomes the author of both good and evil. A good way of saying this is that there is no instrumental cause between God's sovereign will and human free will.

In any case these views are completely theoretical and have nothing to do with the real history of events. They fly in the face of the biblical emphasis that I am guilty only for what I have actually freely done. It contradicts the clear hope of Scripture that there will come a time, not yet here, when a person will bear the responsibilities for his own sin and not also bear the weight of the sin of others (Ezekiel 18). That is not yet our situation. But this scripture does say that we are not all equally guilty, certainly not from conception on, though we are imperfect in a broken nature, being born from an imperfect set of ancestors into a broken world. In God's eyes perfect justice reigns only when guilt and consequences are meted out to the guilty party alone. Being caught in the net of sin spun by others establishes my handicap but not my guilt. I will suffer painful and tragic consequences of other people's choices, but I do not share in their responsibility for them.

Cause and Consequence

In a world of really significant actions we bear the effects of the guilt of other people without being guilty for its cause ourselves. As a German I have to tread gently and carefully with some grief and regret when I travel in Holland. Though I was too young to be a Nazi and though my parents resisted Nazism with considerable cleverness and courage, as a German I bear the consequences of Nazi cruelties and occupation in Holland and a number of other countries.

So we are in a mess. Individually we are guilty in the measure in which we have personally sinned. God keeps a record of that and knows when that happens. That is how real judgment can be administered in the future and real justice can then be established. I believe that human beings are able to establish the guilt of another person both too soon and too late, or not at all. But it is not our business to conclusively judge beyond external evidence and stated intentions, for we do not know the heart of human beings.

In a broken and dangerous world some damaging actions may be provoked by others or by our own frustrations, even by the need to act in order to learn how reality functions. There may well be harmful results. A small child who drops a bowl of food on the floor is not necessarily doing something morally evil. He may just want to discover what happens when he releases his or her fingers: The bowl falls down and the food is on the carpet. As Mummy comes running she now makes a different face, is rather agitated, and the child may feel some pain on the hand or the bottom in the next moment. The experience may not be a choice to do something wrong, but it is part of a valuable and often necessary exploration that ended with a slap. Now the child knows what happens in those circumstances.

I don't know when accountability sets in. God is the judge, and at some point in time we each become guilty. I am not guilty for being a human being. The newly born child is not a moral adult in an underdeveloped body. Having a fallen nature is not the result of my personal guilt. I had no choice in the matter. Choice sets in at a later stage, when creativity gets misused and when a lie is embraced as reality.

But in either case—whether through guilty personal choices or through experiencing life in the fallen world—the fabric of our lives needs purification, correction, and forgiveness. Christ, the Lord of the universe, came to give his life that our guilt would be paid for and that the whole creation would again be restored. The lamb and the lion need the work of Christ as much as a human being, though for different reasons. We need the work of Christ because we have deliberately sinned. We both need it for the removal of the effects of sin in creation. There will be a resurrection for people and a change of behavior for animals and nature.

God, the Interventionist

Sin in the Bible has several related meanings. First it describes moral guilt, when we sin against the holy God by believing, and then often practicing, what is false, empty, wrong, and foolish. There is a real and created world. Any false belief about it, about God or human beings is foolish, inaccurate, unfounded, and wrong, breaking the law of the universe by pretending that something imagined is more real than reality. That is sin in the narrow and specific way. We have all sinned in this way.

But sin also has a second meaning. In a more general sense it stands for any imperfection anywhere that does not reach the mark of what God had in mind when he created reality. Animals are not guilty, but they are under sin. Nature is not accountable; it follows its own regular laws, but it is less now than what God made it to be. It is imperfect throughout.

The Messianic promises all along talk about God's work for soul and body and for creation. Paul says in 1 Corinthians 15 that if Christ is only dead on the cross and not raised again we are still in our sins. That would be only half the work of the Messiah, and there would be no hope for its efficacy, unless there is also a resurrection for humanity and a restoration of all creation. The New Heaven and New Earth will know no conflict, death, or frustration. The New Jerusalem will come down to earth (Revelation 21:1–2) where the evil elements will have been removed through purifying fire and wholeness will be found. It will not all have gone up in smoke (2 Peter 3:10).

That is the work of God, expressed as his grace to us, which shows that God freely favors what he has made and is willing to pay for its restoration. In fact, the grace of God starts when God runs after Adam and Eve in the garden immediately after both had sinned to ask: "Adam, where are you?" Full of shame they hid in the bushes, but God comes after them to urge them to not give up. Their new broken situation will be full of problems, but is not final.

God himself will start to work with them to heal the damage and to provide a real savior for both the moral dilemma of guilt ("God shows his anger from heaven against all sinful, wicked people who push the truth away from themselves." Romans 1:18 NLT) and the external dilemma of death.

For the first element of that promise, they were to wait for that woman among their future descendents who would give birth to the Messiah. For the second element of that promise, they were to put their hand to the plough and work, even though it would now be fraught with difficulties, sweat, and tears. Even in their relationship they would face problems which they must iron out. The man will unhappily, often, rule over the woman. It is important to note that this is a lament, not a command; it is a result of the fall, not a command for marital submission! And the woman will experience more pain in childbirth and rearing. Just look at the real world of human societies to see how broken we are. And notice how cracked and unstable nature is in itself. Third, we notice how much damage humanity and nature do to each other. Harmony has been weakened everywhere.

In this context the promise of God takes on great importance. Things will not always remain the way they have become after sin entered God's good creation. A repair job needs to be undertaken over time. Both God and Man will work for redemption. God's work is both juridical in seeing justice done and material in the renewal of a fallen creation. Adam and Eve at the beginning of the human race are reminded to have children, for though to dust their bodies will return in death, only in the struggle for life that transcends death through children yet to be born will the Messiah come: "And Adam named his wife Eve, for she would become the mother of all the living" (Genesis 3:20).

The situation of our history in the real world from the fall on is of God running after man, of his not accepting the new normality that set in after the fall. It will not remain and thus characterize all of subsequent history. "God, who in his very being is gracious. . . ." is part of the Anglican and Episcopal Liturgy that expresses our hope so well. The God of the Bible is an intervening God, active, creative, pleading, and striving to accomplish his purposes. Life with God is not all smooth sailing. There is opposition from powers, the flesh, and the devil. There are conditional prophecies and promises. There are additional years of wandering in the desert before Israel enters the Promised Land. Christ expressed sorrow when Jerusalem would not respond with belief and joy to his presence and calling.

Climb, then, with me the twin spires of St. Pierre in Geneva. In the nave below, Calvin preached to the citizens in town and to all those who traveled to this free and independent republic that no longer belonged to Savoy nor yet to Switzerland. From up here, next to the mighty bells, you look out over the lake and countryside. To the north and west lay Burgundy, and then further west lay France, to the south the kingdom of Savoy and to the east the poor peasant regions of the Helvetians, the modern Swiss. What will you say to the people below whose exposure to life was intimate, whose experiences were very mixed, and whose social and legal situations were fragile at best. Death by many means was always present. What is different up here from everything that anyone has said before?

Most people were all too familiar with all the unfairness of life and the frequent cruelty of man to his neighbor. Most of the time they were told to see the hand of God in all of it. It served the Church well to make use of common calamities. They served as a reminder that bad choices often lead to destructive consequences. They reveal that something was wrong. But this way of seeing had tragic shortcomings—often it did not give the tools to evaluate life's experiences further. Not all evil is the result of immediate bad choices. Yet the Church readily joined the fellowship of Job's friends in the Old Testament. The ubiquitous mud and early death for hundreds of years were easily assumed as deserved and justified. Hope and righteousness concerned themselves with life after death to be earned through suffering, submission, and resignation here on earth.

When life is understood to be the manifestation of God's will, God becomes part of an overriding unfairness in the lives of individuals. God then becomes an accomplice of death, human wickedness, and incoherent suffering. The innocence of God gets easily muddled when Job's friends surround you on all sides, and you know nothing else. But in God's dealing with Job, his friends did not have the last word. Neither did the Roman church at the time of the Reformers. They found in Scripture the innocence of God and proclaimed it then openly, passionately and with people in mind.

CHAPTER THREE

RELIEF IN THE LAW
OF A JUST GOD

No Longer Victims

You will understand Calvin's heart and mind better when you place yourself into the situation of the sixteenth century than if you approach it as a theological technician. Even the few members of noble families who owned enough not to starve or freeze like most of the peasants working the fields and fishing the lake would frequently be exposed to unsafe roads, diseases, rough treatment, and a harsh life where life expectancy was often little more than twenty-five to thirty years. There were few courts of law and many accidental deaths. All their lives they heard about God, about judgment, and about life after death. They understood God's punishment to be immediate and saw it in sickness, natural disasters, and human cruelty. They grounded their fears in the instructions received from church and accepted as fair whatever happened to them. But they found few places for their little flames of hope and their hunger for life and justice.

With a very short life on earth, life after death became very desirous. It drew people to a hope for something longer, eternal even. But there was the future judgment of God to be feared. On one hand it would bring about what was lacking on earth, where there was little rule of law and frequent exceptions for the noble classes. But it would also bring to the light of day their rather uncivilized behavior. Perceiving divine judgment in events of this life *and* fearing it again in the next haunted people without resolution. Only later in heaven would there be no sickness and death, no demonic power, and no unrewarded sweat and toil as there were now on earth. So the question was: how to get there?

The Roman church at times used words of wrath and promise from Scripture, traditions, and folk tales. It often exploited the poor when it worked in cahoots with the rich in an old conflict spanning centuries over political and economic power, market rights, and spiritual as well as educational growth. It embraced and nurtured many popular superstitions and spoke of Christ's work as though it was only for the deserving. But who is deserving? If it cost you something, can merit be earned by paying for it in food for the clergy, paintings for the churches, and donations for the construction of St. Peter's Cathedral in Rome? Can you book heaven in advance through purchase of redemption tickets in the form of indulgences? How high is the margin to reach salvation? When can deliverance be counted on?

We know the debate over works versus grace. But in reality the question arose out of an increasingly humanistic theology that developed since the Lateran Councils in the twelfth century. That change in theology would in the ensuing decades open a growing chasm between the spiritual people and the common man, the clergy and the manual laborer. Rood screens in the Western church and growing walls of icons in the Eastern and Russian Orthodox churches drew a physical barrier between the "holy deserving" and the common needy parishioners. At that time the priest turned from the people, to whom he had ministered, to the altar to now minister to God. People no longer received the wine of communion for fear that they might spill it. Only the wafer was placed on their tongue. One had to become good enough to merit the merit of Christ without ever really knowing how much was required, where the cut-off line was. One could say that in that Roman theology, sanctification had to precede justification.

And, of course, if there were such a level of sanctification that needed to be reached it would be important to know quite a few things. One would need to know how high it is, also whether it is stable or constantly changing and whether credits towards it would be kept in storage until the sum is reached. Could more credits be accumulated than needed by one person, which could then be traded like modern pollution merits under the Kyoto proposals? But no answer was found in the church, for it could not be found in the Bible. It is a hopeless effort to work with the trick of movable goals. What use is it to know that saying a prayer with full devotion and sincerity before a crucifix in church would give you seven years, three months, five days, and nine hours of release from purgatory when you never know what your total is from which you could deduct this service done? I saw such amounts written in the Old Cathedral in St. Louis, Missouri, in the U.S. and on mission crosses in fields around Southern Germany.

The whole idea of counting up merits must have been some trick, for when the Reformers came with their Bible and taught the finished work of Christ, salvation as a free gift from God to humanity, the people called for the famous Lausanne Disputation between Reformers and clergy in 1526. The town's people listened to both sides presenting their case to see whose views were more grounded in the Bible. Then they voted overwhelmingly with the Reformers, for little of the Church's teaching was based on anything the Bible had to say. Several other cantons in Switzerland introduced the Reformation in some such form by an open consideration of the reasons for faith until the bishops in other cantons saw that they were losing their influence and stopped further debates.

Calvin in Geneva spoke to an audience concerned with such uncertainties about life, God, and salvation. Until then nothing was clear about God's favor or fury, man's place in unstable cir-

cumstances, salvation or hell fire, knowing God and normal daily
life on top of it. Everything was in constant turmoil and under
changing directions.

Roman Catholic teaching had replaced the many gods and
supporting spirits of pagan faith and fear by belief in one God, the
mediation of the "mother of God," and many supporting saints.
But the fear from uncertainty largely remained. Pagan gods were
not seen as kindly or in man's favor. The multitudes of saints on
bridges, in chapels, and on hilltops were more a reminder of a basic uncertainty than tellers of what you could safely count on.

The God of the church's teaching was close to those few people on the other side of the rood screen in their colorful heavenly
vestments. What were the possibilities for the common man with
filthy hands, a sickly body, and constant fear for life and soul at a
time of little access to law, reason, and truth?

Try to place yourself in a world without courts of law, without a public and critical press, without much education, without
security for home and hearth. Imagine a life where you're facing
death from sword or illness all the time, interpreting this as a judgment from God, without certainty about God being good or evil.
It is in this arena that you can feel how thunderously wonderful
the Reformers' teaching from the Bible must have been. Man, for-
merly the victim of divine or natural circumstances, was now addressed by name, with a mind to be informed and to be used. The
Bible's coherent history gave the larger picture of the "where from,
what for, and where to" of all of life. And God was shown to be
in our favor, for the Creator does not abandon his creation. Grace
in the form of judgment for sin already satisfied in Christ was the
new focus, which replaced the old fear that judgment could only
be avoided by unending toil and sacrifice.

In spite of the evidence from your daily lives about the absurdity of much that happens and the fragility of your physical life,
there is one source of truth and wonder. This Source "runs after
you" with a free gift, as God did after Adam. God explains in the

Bible that not all events are deserved. We live in a fallen world now in which things go wrong and where not all pain and death are divine judgements. God has chosen to offer salvation to a world of people in their mess, confusion, guilt, and suffering. That salvation is available to the most terrible sinner, the most depraved soul, the most damaged body.

Law and Love

Calvin gave us a host of insights into the Bible and, going beyond simply theological discussions, preached to people from scriptural insight the need for peace in the city of Geneva. The Greek word for city is *polis*, from which we derive our words for the interrelated realities of "politeness;" where that is lacking we depend on "police;" and where they need direction also "politics." The Bible speaks of good and bad government, true and false prophets, faithful and deceitful priests. It opens our eyes to the need to be more critical and to take a stand for good and moral politics that replace the politics of power.

Calvin, like Farel and Luther and many Reformers, was not only a theologian, but also a lawyer. In fact, part of theology studies at the universities in their day was the study of church and common law. For that reason we still have the double LL, for Liturgical Law, for the basic law degree in our modern setting. The early interest of the Church in education and the founding of numerous universities focused on law, medicine, and classics. In Law you studied canonical law and its common relevance. All such studies nurtured a hunger to understand God and creation in order to bring explanation, logic, and peace to a bleeding people.

Law is always a summary of the shape of reality, both as a reminder of what is and of what should be done to express what we understand to be real, true, and good. That is also the case for the Bible. "To love the Lord your God with all your heart, mind and soul and your neighbor as yourself," is the one great commandment. It is fleshed out in the Ten Commandments at the time of Moses when slavery in Egypt had diluted the understanding and practice of the "great" command. The prophets applied that law to historical, social, and cultural perversions in Israel's history and pronounced impending judgment by God over their failure to love the Lord with all their heart and their neighbors as themselves. The law was given, Paul says, because of added transgression in the flow of time (Galatians 3:26) in order to diminish the acceptance and practice of wrong.

But a lawyer's outlook can easily make things too tight, fitting into a mathematical and quantitative mode that neglects the "soft" realities of love, generosity, and compassion. It is not that these oppose law or logic, but they complete what justice is also concerned about in the complexities of life. Justice is more than legal precision. Law is a teacher to inform, not a tool to induce compliance. A concern for justice includes also the reality that we are persons to be served, not objects to be shoved about; that we relate in thought and by choices rather than that we just exist and have a title. The Bible reveals such a complex justice as flowing from God and admonishes us to practice it.

Some lawyers at the time of Jesus could not understand that justice is more than an eye for an eye or that the guilt of murder or adultery can be present on the basis of intent alone. We call this the subjective side of guilt and merit. It deals with a person's motivation before any action takes place. The Sermon on the Mount addresses the difficulty of judging invisible intent from the outside with a call for greater personal righteousness, which is nothing less than each of us figuring out before the living God what is "right," factual, real, and true in any situation. The Pharisees had rules and regulations, but our righteousness should result from thought, wisdom, and prayer, from love and creative effort.

Now a person's need for a shirt should be met with generosity, because he is a human being who does not come equipped at birth with a coat of fur as a part of his development. Jonah should have had compassion on the terrible sinners of Nineveh and been glad for their repentance. David was right to eat of the untouchable bread when he was hungry after doing the Lord's business. Is it evil to do good work on the Sabbath? Is law made for man or man for the law?

Calvin's Rediscovery

Calvin is perhaps best known to a wider public within and without the Church for the way he restated God's relationship to believers through grace in predestination. For some he is the great saint who rightly reaffirmed the central theme of the whole Bible found in the grace of God and his covenant. It is the unconditional gift of God, in which he shows himself to be in our favor from the beginning. Here he reveals in history his true character. In his very being our God is gracious. Grace is not an afterthought or a decision on Tuesday at noon. God offers forgiveness as a consequence of the work of the Messiah, "from before the foundation of the world."

For others, Calvin is at times the villain of the Reformation, an autocrat in Geneva's government with a low view of people whom he saw as depraved in sin and hopelessly lost except for the certain number who were chosen or predestined by God to redemption. In many people's minds the word "predestination" is almost automatically related to Calvin in Geneva. Francis Schaeffer always questioned the wisdom of Calvin to create a new civic society rather than to focus on the power of biblical teaching to change human behavior. For that reason he called his study center *Farel House* after the preacher of the countryside. Today most Protestants avoid such reflections and accept predestination as God's determined action in the lives of people.

The advantage of such a view is a profound certainty about events in history and an affirmation of one's convictions. It easily allows people to see themselves as special and distinct from others in their calling from God. It also suggests the possibility of judgment on the basis of life's experiences and, by extension, on their success in life. "Chosen by God" will become visible and work itself out in self-confidence, certitude, and success which are at times distinguished, only with great effort and sensitivity, from selfishness, pride, and a roughness towards other human beings who are not elect in God's predestination.

The disadvantage of such a view of being among the chosen is that there is little room for admitting and dealing with complexity, with failure, and with something less than perfection while maintaining the "call of God." Failure or feeling of failure in life will easily lead to an unexamined sense of guilt, rejection, and loss of a sense of worth. The reasoning at times goes something like this: God would not want his chosen ones to have a miserable life. Ergo, if your life is miserable, you must be guilty and deserve it. Your experiences confirm that you are totally depraved and unworthy of God's love, therefore you may not be one of the elect.

Psychologists deal with causes of depression and a sense of hopelessness; not surprisingly, too many cases involve people with a background of Calvinistic teaching about depravity and election. They easily have a sense of failure when life gets tough. In our social and cultural context, this sense expresses itself in an inability to admit failure, to seek advice and help. When the feeling reaches an extreme isolation it often leads to suicide. What is the use of even trying if the perfect standard, identified with the calling of God, cannot be reached?

The only other way to respond to such feelings is to get rid of God or oneself. Many people have chosen the former when they become atheists; fewer people choose the latter, yet Switzerland, the original home of the reformers, has one of the highest suicide rates in the western world. Suicide is the highest cause of death among teenagers.

It is interesting that Japan has the same problems occurring when people are unable to satisfy the divine standard set by

"Shinto." Failure to keep up with the expectations of the group, the nation, and the company, (all of which manifest a divine order and purpose in this understanding) often leads to black depression and a loss of place, which then results in the loss of a life seen as unworthy.

Calvin did not invent the term "predestination," and it should not be the first concept or word that comes to mind when the Geneva Reformer is mentioned or discussed. It is a term used a number of times in the Bible. It indicates that God has made a choice in our favor and will see it through. He will pay for salvation and give it freely to those who believe that it is true instead of calling God a liar. The Bible's understanding of faith is "being sure of what we hope for and certain of what we do not [yet] see. . . . Anyone who comes to [God] must believe that he exists and that he rewards those who earnestly seek him" (Hebrews 11:1; 6).

Predestination is the Bible's response to the uncertainties of life and the frivolities found among people, including people who teach and direct churches. Rather than living under unknown fates or irrational circumstances, Calvin rightly taught that there is a God who has made a choice. Predestination, we shall see, describes that choice by God in our favor. It is exhibited numerous times in God's dealing with Israel, with Christians, and with people seeking to know if there is a good God in such a crazy and unfair world as ours. This crazy and sinful world, taken alone, would justify anyone not believing that this could be the work of a good God. Too much evil has neither rhyme nor reason; "All is vanity."

In Calvin's historical and social context, Scripture's predestination refers to a choice God made to offer us salvation, so that whoever believes in the Son has everlasting life (John 3:16). This is a genuine "whosoever," unless things are not what they appear to be or words do not mean what they seem to say. Surely they need to be placed in connection with whole sentences, which are part of complete texts. The Bible was not written as a collection of unconnected sayings. It is not a quarry for the quote of your preference. These are letters from God, in which a case is made for God, for humanity, for reason and facts and, above all, for discernment between truth and falsehood, between imaginings and reality. Arguments are elaborated and clarified. In addition, each letter adds to the previous ones so that a whole structure of understanding is set up. The God of the Bible wants us to know his favorable intervention for us.

Texts need to be studied, not simply quoted. You need to find out, as in any text, what could be meant, what could not possibly be meant, what is not being said, and what is said and argued for. Inspiration from God, assumed and taught in the Bible, and full reliability of the Bible, discovered in studies across many disciplines, does not preclude hard work to understand the text. The Bible constantly disarms simplistic assumptions by providing insight that eventually becomes obvious. It sheds light on reality and shows that there is no gap between what is and what seems to be. Words have precise and consistent meaning in their context. God challenges us to examine his truth in relation to reality, history, and time. Only then should we believe it. Paul defends himself against false accusations of having preached for personal gain and fame with deceptive words (See 1 Thessalonians and 2 Corinthians). Jesus demands that people check what he says against what they see and know from past prophecies (Matthew 11).

In daily sermons, Calvin was reaching out to anxious and confused people to tell them good news: rather than humans having to reach an undetermined standard of merit, God forgives when we acknowledge that he is right about everything—himself, us, and the problems we have caused. God has maintained the standard of his perfection and accomplished justice through the perfect work of Christ. When the Messiah, the Anointed One, became sin for us in his death, he was separate from the Father for us. He took the consequences of our sin and suffered them for us. He maintained the standard and paid the price for guilt in full. The passion of

Christ is not so much his suffering from fellow humans, but from being rejected by God the Father for the time he bore our transgressions on the tree.

Isaiah 59 promises this concern of God and his commitment to undertake steps for our salvation in the Old Testament. "Surely the arm of the Lord is not too short to save, nor his ear too dull to hear," he says. "But your iniquities have separated you from your God; your sins have hidden his face from you, so that he will not hear" (verses 1–2). After the list of sins a summary concludes in verses 14 and 15 with, "So justice is driven back, and righteousness stands at a distance; truth has stumbled in the streets, honesty cannot enter. Truth is nowhere to be found, and whoever shuns evil becomes a prey." But it is not hopeless, for "the Lord looked and was displeased that there was no justice. He saw that there was no one, he was appalled that there was no one to intervene; so his own arm worked salvation for him, and his own righteousness sustained him" (15–16). After judgment of sins, "'the Redeemer will come to Zion, to those in Jacob who repent of their sins,' declares the Lord" (20).

The judge of the universe who points out our guilt decides to pay for it himself so that we could be freed from guilt. Faith is the response of the creature to the truth in history, law, and anthropology.

Therefore even the greatest sinner can receive pardon. It is available unconditionally and not dependent on one's goodness. God set out a single and sufficient way for each of us, so that no one needs to be lost, for God does not desire alienation for anyone (1 Timothy 2:4). What God had set out to do, each member of the Trinity actively pursues. God's investment for us in the payment of his Son's death for our sin will bear eternal fruit, as God perseveres and will complete what he has started.

This is the grace of God in Christ, according to the Bible. It remains for us to respond when we learn of what God has done.

We seek answers to the questions of existence. Who are we? What are we here for? Who says what is right anyway? How do we know which religion is true? To these and all the other important questions of the human race only the Bible gives answers in such a way that they make sense within themselves and in relation to the common world which we all share. There is an internal consistency of mutually supportive affirmations. But there is also an external consistency with all reality, including the human being. There is no final conflict between what the Bible affirms and what reality confirms.

Paul writes to the church in Thessalonica with praise, for they "turned from [many confusing, competing, and invented] idols to the true and living God" (1 Thessalonians 1:9). This God is "true" because you can argue with him and challenge his statements, acts, and promises to see whether they stand the test of history, logic, and fact. He is "living" in that he speaks with words that can be checked, that carry clear meaning and relate to the most common human experiences. He must be a God of passions and emotions, of laughter and tears, of sadness and disappointments and power. Only the God of the Bible is such a God.

Where human beings in Greece were always exposed to the tragic reality of what the fates and gods were doing, the God of the Bible is innocent of the human predicament. He created a good world. After humanity's fall and estrangement, God has continuously gone to great effort to not be identified with all events in history. Some events are of human creation, others are a part of a broken world after the fall. There are also the overlapping results from Satan roaming about "looking for someone to devour" (1 Peter 5:8). We have much cause to demand justice from God. He is not in the seat of the accused, but in the judge's chair.

CHAPTER FOUR

GOD PRESENT IN HISTORY, BUT WHERE?

Yahweh, Unlike Greek Fates

Calvin's views were often taken out of their original historic and cultural context. Evolving systems of theology were established with lawyers' minds and often without the compassion that was part of Calvin's life and work in Geneva. New views were embraced and texts altered by Calvin's students to fit these new viewpoints. The sensibility and coherence of Christianity was fitted into the rationalistic philosophical delights of the seventeenth century. The study of Greek philosophers encouraged a desire to have Christian theology be the answer to their quest. But instead of broadening the questions, the responses were narrowed. Christians should have recognized that Greek philosophers asked insufficient questions in their search for the "ideal." Instead, many theologians squeezed the personal-infinite God of the Bible into Greek expectations. They reduced the passionate and dynamic character of God into that of a deterministic sovereign.

The field of mechanics revealed perhaps the first social benefit from the scientific study of an ordered universe. Clocks, the camera obscura, absolutist monarchies, and economic mercantilism reveal a common thread connecting them: the delight in having clear and fixed answers. On the positive side, the uncertainties of superstition were reduced. But the goal of seeking the recently rediscovered pleasures of rationality became paramount. Everything now had to be resolved at once to protect the God they believed in and themselves.

Theology as well became a vehicle in this drive to rationalize. Calvin's disciples handled his teaching in a way disciples often do: they reduce complex realities to simple formulas. I remember hearing the Dutch philosopher Herman Dooyeweerd saying "what the master thought, his disciples turned into absolute truth." Many Calvinists, like religious determinists elsewhere, sought to leave no stone unturned; they wished to put all reality into a closed system under God. They ended up with something else, leaving no turn of life "un-stoned." They threw their judgment zealously at any evidence of human struggle to understand how a good God could be in willful and sovereign control of a broken world. Jesus had similar problems with disciples who at some times were "ye of little faith" and at other times sought to keep children and others not with them from coming to Jesus—even when this latter group spoke favorably of Christ.

Neither Calvin nor any other person is the final expositor of Scripture. It is quite evident that he did not make "election" a central doctrine. He was not concerned with a resolute systematic theology of unambiguous and consistent ideas hermetically sealed in a mold of airtight logic. Because of this, he would not stress any one doctrine as the basis of his theology. There is perhaps much more variety and subtlety to his thought than was admitted by his disciples who became craftsmen of something less than biblical wholeness. They reveal an anxious drive for consistency; he a surprising resourcefulness that may well have been his response to the needs of his parishioners.

It is easy to forget that doctrine must not become doctrinaire. Yet this happened when "predestination" was pushed forward to where "destiny" previously had answered the control question in uncertain and questionable moral circumstances of life. But with that change no better answer was given, for the moral question about who is in charge of a contradictory, wicked, and painful life remained unanswered in areas in which no direct moral and factual connection exists between cause and effect. Pointing to the sinfulness of men and women to explain so much tragedy and pain is one thing. But to see all of it as a matter of cause and effect, as normal and in some way therefore as good and desired by the Sovereign either makes him evil or our perceptions perverse.

Predestination also became a way to explain why some people believe and others do not. God had chosen to do something for some and not for others, without explaining why there is a mess to start with. Some had simply received faith or something from God and others had not. The Holy Spirit regenerated those selected, while not raising others from the common spiritual death for which we were responsible before we were able to think and act. That appears to be a neat but deadly, system. It is like the millstone Jesus speaks about in Matthew 18:6 that will also drown teachers who keep people from coming to believe. But now it is tied to those who seek to know. They are told that their search is hopeless, they are unable even to seek; it is all a matter of predestination from God alone.

Happily, this has nothing to do with what the Bible brings us concerning God's word and work in history. For while this view has all the appearance of a neat system and gives tight explanations of all kinds of things happening, it is precisely only that: neat. But it is not clean, coherent, or scriptural. It is impersonal, seemingly arbitrary, but in any case not moral. It is in no way respectful of human beings, who did not choose to even be born in the first place.

God's respect for his unfaithful bride, Israel (seen in Hosea and other prophetic writings), pleading with her to return, is a far more obvious and repeated expression of God's way of dealing with his sinful creation.

There is no room in the rigidly deterministic system associated with Calvinism for real personality in either God or humanity. In fact, it parallels the fatalistic views of other religions. Man is always the victim of higher powers and more dominant forces of longer duration. Whether you name this Allah or God, energy or extraterrestrials, stars, ancestors, or history, in each case this view leaves you in an impersonal universe. The passion of Christ is then contrived, the labor of the Apostles mere play-acting, the apologetics of the church merely a piece of theater with a prepared script. There is no Yahweh left, once God is seen as the puller of levers who predestines this or that, whatever.

Calvin's disciples were not the first to envision such a God and to advocate such a one-sided source of history, where only one actor pulls all the strings. As we shall see, the Bible does not teach this—if it did, it would be out of reach of critical evaluation and would have to be believed blindly and stupidly, without the possibility of examination. "Come now, let us reason together," God's words to Isaiah in Isaiah 1:18, would be a silly phrase if humankind were unable to recognize reality, did not have choices with consequences, options between alternatives and insights for the evaluation of what is good, just, and beautiful.

The early church already fell to the Greek and Gnostic temptation, and Paul wrote against these repeatedly. I am confident that the Apostolic writing is not the fruit of their knowledge of Greek thought. That idea was a proposition of nineteenth century scholarship long since disproved. The New Testament authors speak for God and from revelation, not for idols or from Greek philosophic reflection. They lived in a Roman and Greek environment, but at a critical distance from it in a conceptual world informed by Hebrew Scripture, thought, and expectations. There is an important distinction here. In the New Testament, we are faced with a completely different worldview about man and God, about time and knowledge, about history and meaning. We saw in the last chapter how Paul's teaching in Thessalonica had overturned the Greek philosophic horizon by turning his audience from idols to the true and living God, by giving them a sense of purposeful history, an expectation of life after death, and a realization that we live in a moral universe under the judgment of God.

But in the next few generations in the Church, the Gnostic temptations became stronger. Perhaps the desire to meet halfway softened the distinctions between Jerusalem and Athens, between Greek absolute forms and God's eternal existence in holiness. In our own time, we find many who suggest that Islam lacks only faith in Jesus to become the same as Christianity. Yet the difference is not only in Jesus, but in the nature and character of Allah and Yahweh. From the determination of divine character flow various views about truth, humanity, history, meaning, and life itself.

Free From the Fetters of Fate

Let me now return to the blurring of biblical views by an effort to conform to the expectations of the surrounding culture. Related to the discussion about predestination, the Greeks had their Fates, which controlled even what the gods did. Some apologists in the second century tried to appeal to the all-knowing God of the Bible as the equivalent of what the Greeks sought with their unknown fates. God, they said, is perfect. Perfection requires total knowledge, where nothing is ever added. Perfect knowledge requires that nothing will happen that is not known and therefore fixed ahead of time. If God knows everything, people cannot do anything new or original. Therefore God does it all according to his knowledge. God controls what happens in history.

The knowledge of God requires, in this view, the occurrence of events. But that idea is fatalism and not consistent with the God of the Bible in either Old or New Testaments. Yahweh knows all kinds of things that will not happen, because other personages will make their own known choices to prevent things from happening. David's reaction to the announcement from a knowing God that citizens of Keilah (1 Samuel 23:7) will hand him over to his enemy Saul makes it impossible for the events to ever occur—because David, of course, runs away. Thanks to God he knew what would happen if he sat still. Not being a fool, he runs away from what God told him would happen, and so, as God already knew, it never happens.

We shall consider later flaws in that argument about God's omniscience and how different the God of the Bible is from the idea of divine perfection in Greek paganism. The God of the Bible is not "perfection" as an ideal. Only his character and what he does and thinks are free from flaws. In his knowledge there are no voids. God created a real world with a real history, containing real personages that create new situations, all of which God knows. Yet events and personalities do not happen under divine approval when evil is created.

Think of it: God did not create everything at once. He took some time, six days of whatever length, we are told. After a day of rest he creates more all along real history, such as when he took five loaves and two fish and made lunch for five thousand people as recounted in John 6. But more than that, God did not create everything that now exists. He gave the mandate to create more and more variety to humanity. Man gave names to the animals; God did not! Adam and Eve created their relationship; God did not! Man and woman create babies; God does not. Humanity created sin on earth; God did not!

The God of the Bible is not the god of the Greeks, nor is he Allah of Islam or the puppeteer in heaven or the underlying energy of the universe. He is not like some giant personal magnet hidden under a pane of glass, on the surface of which metal splinters follow all the movements, seemingly by themselves, but in fact blindly following the pull of the magnet below.

In fact, all pagan cultures have their forces, spirits, and ghosts, their god or gods or simple energy relations behind all occurrences in history. Greeks, Romans, Germanic tribes, and African and Siberian animism all have in common that someone or something is behind the events we see and participate in. Nothing is left to the creative originality of the creature. There is no freedom, for everything is tied together in the unseen reality behind the seen. The human being is always the victim, which is why there is tragedy: no matter what you choose or do, the outcome is always controlled from somewhere else.

God's Choice: It Ain't What You Think It Is
(Or, No God Behind This Messy Life)

The word "predestined" is used in several places in the Bible, but with quite a different meaning from how it is popularly used to suggest the totality of God's actions. We need to look at them in their context to see this.

Paul uses "predestination" at the end of a teaching that runs through all preceding chapters and ends in Romans 8 in a summary, a doxology to God's faithfulness in contrast to the sin of man. Paul's letter describes the mess we are in and how we got there. Yet God, in spite of all we do, has prepared a way to end both our foolishness in rebellion and his wrath over our sin through the one savior, Jesus Christ. With his Holy Spirit we are living as God's children in the hope of glory, anticipating and living out the gradual repair to wholeness. We're not there yet, but we are not alone, not without truth and strength while we groan in the midst of a damaged reality, enabled to resist sin and evil.

Francis Schaeffer's studies on the first eight chapters of Romans explain the Father's wrath and sorrow that we have become so foolish in our sin (Romans 1:18–32), whether we're Gentiles in the inconsistencies to our own standards (2:1–5) or Jews in our disobedience to God's law in the available text (2:17–29). Both are guilty in reference to their own absolutes. God does not hold them to the same requirements, but both are morally guilty, and they know it! After the accusation, we are told how God can be just to condemn us and at the same time also be the one who justifies, for he has taken the judgment with its consequences on himself (3:21–31). That is the same salvation for Old and New Testament. God's followers of old believed what was yet to happen; we believe what has happened in the past. Both believe the work of God in the Messiah Jesus (Romans 4).

In Romans, Paul continues to talk about the present work of Christ, in whose death we are baptized so that we should reckon ourselves dead to sin (chapters 5 and 6); and the power of the Spirit helps us in the battle against sin in the midst of all kinds of situations, in which we groan in agony, but look forward to glory to be revealed in history (chapters 7 and 8). All the mess now, part of creation's frustration, pain, and very real decay and bondage (8:20–21), will not hinder what God has yet in mind for us. He does not approve of all this, but neither is he resigned to it or in any way incapacitated by it. Instead, since Christ came to work for us, who can be against us? God is working for those who love him (both Gentile and Jew), who have been called according to his purpose. For those God foreknew he also predestined (8:28–30).

In the flow of the letter to the Romans this speaks about God's battle to redeem anyone. The purposes of God are to give redemption through the work of Christ. He knows each person and has set out that which is necessary to make this possible in spite of whatever horrible circumstances are placed in the way by us and by others. But notice that God speaks here, after Romans 5:1, to believers, not to the human race as a whole. The decision to believe or not to believe is made by the time you come to Romans 5:1. Paul confirms God's determination to follow through with those who trust in God. Paul does not say how they came to faith or that God selected some for salvation and rejected others.

The other, more common view of predestination, describes our shopping habits and political choices, but not the acts of God. We select, for manifold and often hidden reasons, one model fridge over another, to eat out or to tithe in church, to marry one person rather than another, and to talk to a cat as a silent presence rather than to have children who interrupt. That is "selection" and is absent from the biblical idea of predestination.

Even Abraham was not selected in such a way, "shopped" from among the entire human race to become the father of many nations and the carrier of the Lord's messianic blessing. He was not chosen for salvation in Genesis 12, for he must already have believed in the God of heaven. In his social context everyone else believed in pagan deities of land and water and seasons of the year. Yet Abram believed that God spoke instructions rather than have him glean them from the community or hear them in the whispers of the wind. He did not follow the Ugaritic Epic, in which people listen to the "speech of the tree and whisper of the stone." He believed that the mind is involved in understanding God, not primarily experiences or feelings or a sense of community.

Abraham chose to follow God's promises about Israel's hope about the coming exclusive savior for all people and nations. It was repeated where the text, even before it was written down, was believed more than the myths. Abel believed this knowledge in contrast to his brother Cain; Noah believed it though his neighbors did not. Psalm 19 beautifully reminds us that nature is magnificent and speaks the language of order, power, and glory. But "there is no utterance, there are no words, whose sound goes unheard." It does not speak. For speech we require more, the law of God, his ordinances, precepts, the teaching of the Lord that renews life (v. 8ff.). Language, not experience, informs Abraham and us about purpose, and words of promise lay the foundation for hope in real history.

The doxology at the end of Romans 8 states God's whole commitment to our salvation and glorification (resurrection and wholeness). Nothing will be able to foil this. The comfort lies in God's commitment to himself, his victory over present and very real and despicable adversity. We do not live in a safe or good world, but God has committed himself to deliver salvation for our guilt and glory for a new creation in the resurrection.

It would be unconscionably wrong to read into the single word "predestined" a form of selection for some and a rejection of others. "Those whom he foreknew" in the same context must not be seen as fitting into the Greek idea of God's perfection, but rather in the Jewish sense of a dynamic history. Of course God knows all things and people and their choices. But the knowledge of God is not a mechanism in any form of controlled events. That was the case for paganism, for views about fate and destiny. But it is foreign to the biblical understanding.

Already in the next chapter of Romans, many teachers find more evidence for their view of God's choice of individuals in the affairs of faith and salvation. Romans 9 through 11 form a separate section in Paul's letter. They treat remaining issues that need clarification. Until now Paul has dealt with the problem of rebellion for the whole human race, the one savior from God, the hope of glory in spite of the present evidence of suffering, death, and frustration to the contrary. Just as Romans 1–8 ends with a doxology to the praise of God, so chapter 11 ends with exuberant doxology.

Again we have a whole treatment or discussion of questions, not just verses to pick and choose to your liking. Paul did not state what he liked. This is not of personal interest only. He did not write to Rome in the way a child may do a "show and tell" in class. Paul addressed the *common* human dilemma and the *single* solution in the first eight chapters of his letter to the Christians in Rome. In what follows he dealt with a distinction that was thought to have some significance. It still exists and is in no way diminished by the discussion relating to common guilt and the common savior.

Why Jacob and Not Esau?

In Romans chapter nine, Paul raises that distinction as a serious question that remains after understanding the first section in chapters 1–8. There he had clearly said that both Jew and Gentile are in the same mess. They are both under God's wrath, because both have sinned and are guilty. Their one hope of salvation is in Christ's finished work. "What then is so special about the Jews?" and "Why did God choose the Jews?" are the questions Paul now answers. They persist. They deal with history.

I have always received a certain amount of pleasure as a German to say that I believe what Abraham believed, with the one difference that he looked forward in time to what I look backward to. I then add that Abraham seems to have been a lone believer among Noah's descendents who did not fall into the trap of pagan fatalism or animism.

Jews would ask this question themselves, since the core of their whole experience and faith is that God spoke primarily to them and not to others. Paul affirms this and lists all kind of things that were special to the Jews, of whom he was one (Romans 9:3–5). Yet "not all who are descended from Israel are Israel (9:6)." He continues with this to point out that what mattered was trust in God's promise of a savior, just as Abraham believed both before Isaac's conception and when he was prepared to sacrifice him about twenty years later, knowing that this would not mean the end of Isaac. Instead God would "provide himself a sacrifice," and the ram was caught in the thicket for Abraham's knife (Genesis 22).

It is in the following curious passage about Jacob and Esau (Genesis 9:10–15) where many find an anchor for their view that God chooses some for salvation and others for condemnation for reasons known only to his own immutable, wise, and inscrutable counsel. Jacob receives the "yes," Esau the "no."

Now that should raise some questions for both believers and non-believers. For the former it raises the question about God's justice: what is this wise, immutable counsel to which we are not privy except in its consequences? How reliable are the words of God in any area, if such a centrally important choice over eternal salvation is not subject to review or normal standards of rationality or justice? The non-believer would rightfully ask why he would be held accountable in matters in which he does not have a choice in any case. He would wonder about that if he were kindly disposed towards God. More justified would be the response that with such a God one does not want to have anything to do anyway. As a student in our house once remarked: "If God is not also Aunt Sophie's savior (who sought the truth all her life), then he is no one's savior!"

As you follow along you will notice again that in Romans chapter nine Paul is not at all talking about individuals being saved. He is talking about what is special about the Jews, when all people, both Gentile and Jew, have sinned (in the past) and fall short of God's perfect standard (in the present). The text "Jacob I loved, but Esau I hated" (v. 13) is a quote from Malachi 1:2–3 which is the last book of the Old Testament, written around one thousand years after the boys had their struggles. It addresses the people of Israel, not Jacob the person who stole the birthright from Esau for mixed reasons. Esau showed in many ways that he was not at all interested in the things of God. He treated the birthright lightly to satisfy a momentary hunger and broke the family pattern when he married Hittite wives.

I find no way to get around this focus on the Jews as distinct from the Edomites in Romans 9, unless you pick and choose the verses you like for your prior theological program or denominational affiliation, then read them without any regard for what is said in those verses as part of a flowing proposition. Paul did not write in isolated verses; he penned a coherent letter meant to be taken in context. The Bible is not like a quarry where we pick various stones to construct what we wish to see.

God is saying something very specific and quite different from what many would like to find here: Israel, in contrast to Esau and the Edomites, was chosen to be the carrier of the promised Messiah. The Messiah was born to the nation of Israel in the tribe of Judah, son of Jacob, in the house of David, from the virgin Mary through no merit of her own in Bethlehem to be the Savior made available to all nations. That is the Abrahamic Covenant again.

The choice of Jacob over Esau proceeds from the promise of the solution from sin and the fall by God, who grieves over what creatures have done with his creation. He remains innocent of their choices but engaged in their redemption. He chooses to commit himself to fully redeem a people who seek to know him. People would be made up of many nations, but the Messiah would come from a Jewish woman. He would not be born from Germans or Tibetans. He would not be found in a Lotus flower, but his ancestor would be rescued in a basket among the reeds that line the Nile. God, who invested so much of himself in his creation, is not ready to abandon it for any reason, ever.

CHAPTER FIVE

PREDESTINATION AND DETERMINISM

Pharaoh Must Blame Himself

The statement, "Jacob I loved, but Esau I hated," in Paul's discussion with the church in Rome is not the only one whose misinterpretation leads to a flawed understanding of God's work on our behalf. Such distortions can happen in many places when an ideology, such as a narrow view of divine sovereignty, is taken as a measure of the text rather than letting the text speak for itself. There are two other references to the Old Testament in this same ninth chapter of Romans that are squeezed to support a particular view of God's sovereignty over people and history. Just as in the first, the next two references to God's hand in our salvation do not point to a selection process or to the salvation of individuals. Both quotations reveal the mercy of God to the people of Israel for the sake of our salvation by faith in the coming Christ. By this mercy God delivered Israel out of Egyptian slavery. By the same mercy God sent prophets to bring Israel repeatedly to repentance.

Again, let us look to see from where Paul quotes these illustrations. After all, the Old Testament was his book of God's word. In the first citation Paul refers to Israel's deliverance from slavery in Egypt, which is described in great detail in Exodus. Paul would expect his audience in Rome to be familiar with this central event in Israel's history to which the prophets and the Psalmist refer frequently and which is commemorated in the yearly Passover Feast anticipating the death of the Lamb of God.

Pharaoh had his heart hardened, just as God promised Moses in his fear and hesitation. But again, just as in God's earlier distinction of Israel, God's dealing with Pharaoh is not a freak event of divine mind control while Pharaoh had his mind on other things, perhaps sitting among his date palms or visiting yet another palace built by Israelite slave labor. The record in Exodus shows how several plagues fell over Egypt before Pharaoh insisted with finality that he would not "let my people go." Early on he had already lost the support amongst his diviners, who gradually realized that they could no longer counter the powerful and terrible miracles of God. They urged Pharaoh to back off, but he would not. Just as a post planted into cement can be moved for a while before the cement hardens, so Pharaoh's heart hardened more with each plague until the Lord said something like, " That's it, enough. Now there is no more movement in the mud, no more backing out of the grave you have dug yourself."

God promised that he would harden Pharaoh's heart (Exodus 4:21; 7:3), just as he promised to give Moses courage (3:12), a speaker in his brother Aaron (4:10–17), and miracles such as the snake turning into a staff (4:1–9).

Yet the text does not recount God's hardening Pharaoh's heart until Exodus 9:12. Each of the plagues of blood, flies, gnats, boils, and hail left Pharaoh still with a choice. But his heart became hard; he would not even listen to Moses and Aaron in 7:13 and 22. In 8:15 it is clearly Pharaoh's choice to harden his heart, for he had bargained with Moses for prayer. The next day when relief came, Pharaoh broke his promise to let the people go (8:8–14). In 8:32

we are told that "this time also Pharaoh hardened his heart and would not let the people go."

Only in 9:12 after all the preceding plagues does the text say that "the Lord hardened Pharaoh's heart," echoing this refrain after the two remaining plagues of locusts and of darkness. Pharaoh backed himself into a position where there was no way out. After that Pharaoh only pretends to repent, not even asking for deliverance prayer anymore (9:27ff.). As soon as the plague of hail stopped Pharaoh "sinned again: He and his officials hardened their hearts" (34).

Hardening Pharaoh's heart was no unconditional act of God. This was no divine zapping with a curse, no undeserved judgment out of the blue sky for some superior divine purpose, or an example of lightening striking some innocent person along a country road. Instead you see a gradually stiffer determination in Pharaoh to resist, even hiding it behind religious acts by asking for prayer and finally pretending to believe, yet contradicting everything previously expressed. This is deliberate on the part of Pharaoh and reminds me much more of what the sins against the Holy Spirit, spoken of in the New Testament by Jesus, must involve.

The people of Egypt, in contrast to their ruler, were favorably disposed toward God's people so that when the Israelites left they did not go empty-handed (Exodus 3:21; 11:2).

"What then shall we say? Is God unjust? Not at all!" (Romans 9:14) At no time was Pharaoh in a locked position until his previous and very significant choices made it impossible to get back to the start. There never is a sign that even then he wished it to be different but could no longer repent because of something God had done. He just chose repeatedly not to let the people go and therefore had to go himself. What court would have listened to his complaint?

People are Not Made of Clay

In the second Old Testament illustration Paul refers to the repeated sending of the prophets to Israel to encourage, reproach, and admonish the people to apply God's law faithfully. Yet they fell back into unfaithfulness, hypocrisy, and human cruelty without regard to the commandments. Here in Romans 9:21 and the passages that follow. Paul uses an illustration, found in both Jeremiah and Isaiah, from the relation between the potter and the pot to describe the struggle of God with Israel. If the pot is not rightly formed it will be condemned. For the potter has the right to see that it will turn out well.

Isaiah 29:16 clearly establishes that the potter set the form for the clay, even though Israel in rebellion thought they could forget God and form their own laws for society. God's people "worked in the dark"; they said, "Who sees us? Who will know?" when Israel said that God has not made them (29:15–16). But in a little while the humble would obtain fresh joy in the Lord, the deaf would hear the words of a scroll or book, and out of their gloom and darkness the blind would see. The poor would exult in the Holy one of Israel (vv. 17–19).

In Jeremiah 18 the same picture of potter and pot is used to explain why God has a right to judge Israel in its rebellion. The work of God did not turn out right. It is not perfect and can perfectly well be destroyed by the will of the potter.

Yet it is remarkable that in both instances, as well as in Isaiah 64, the picture serves to illustrate the moral reasons for destruction but does not justify the destruction itself. It clarified the legal right, not its execution. For both in Isaiah and in Jeremiah the threat of destruction, punishment, and death is made to reach people for repentance. God treats people as people and not as a thing like a pot. God is just to condemn what is marred through sin and therefore has not turned out as intended. But the flaw in the pot did not come from the potter's hands or his failures, but from an impurity in the clay. Israel did not turn out right through a design flaw or some eternal will of God. Both pot and people deserve judgment.

But here the parallel ends. The illustration from pot and potter establishes the right to destroy what has no life. The parallel in God's relation to people stops, however, with the dissatisfaction to continue into a plea for the peoples' repentance. The illustration, as always later in the parables of Jesus, must be seen for the point it tries to make. It has to be taken with a grain of salt and is not a plan for execution. In the illustration the point is the potter's right to demand perfection of his work. A pot is an impersonal object made from clay under the molding hand of the potter. He selects the clay, kneads it and gives it shape. It may not turn out, and the potter has the right to start again.

But in God's relation to Israel, the people—who had been made without flaw—rebel and make themselves imperfect. The good marriage between God as groom and Israel as bride was violated by the adultery of the bride. Israel's choice produces the problem; their repentance needs to restore the relationship. Again and again that is what happened as God intended until the people sinned again.

To extend the purpose of this picture and include in it some kind of divine determinism is not in the text. The Isaiah and Jeremiah passages both employ this image to drive home the urgent need for people to *act now*, not to be acted upon without their participation. God sent prophets to the people when they did not live up to God's standards, so that they would repent. God treats people as capable people, choice-makers, significant and responsible. He never treats people as sticks or stones, or, to stay within the analogy, as clay pots.

Paul answers the questions about the Jews throughout Romans 9. They were selected, preserved, and corrected throughout their history since Abraham in order to be the people from whom the Messiah would be born. Romans 9 does not deal with individual salvation, a process of selecting some and rejecting others. It does not deal with God's right to destroy if he wants, or to act into history regardless of people to get things done. Romans 9 shows how through Israel's God a cornerstone is laid in Zion "that causes men to stumble and a rock that makes them fall, and the one who trusts in him will never be put to shame" (33).

Israel must believe (though not all did and were therefore not a part of spiritual Israel; see Romans 9:6) as must we, with zeal, but also according to the truth (10:2) which comes by hearing (10:14–17). "For God's gifts and his call are irrevocable" (11:29).

The Roots of Corruption

The Bible therefore presents us with quite a different, dynamic understanding of history that needs to be shouted out over the roofs of Thessalonica and Geneva, into the minds of people who have always in the past been told that some fate, some god or spirits, some abstraction like 'history' or tradition, some physical or psychological influence controlled their lives. Neither gods nor party programs, neither nature nor traditions make a prison for heart and mind and body so tight that humankind ceases to bear the image of God with a mandate to create, discover, debate, and believe for good and moral reasons. Anything ideology or theology that denies this truth does not draw its life from the Bible, but is instead an open grave. "For everyone who calls on the name of the Lord will be saved" (Romans 10:13). One does not become such an "everyone" by some exclusive selection process.

Only the desire to find pleasure in one's preconceived theology can make one so particularly blind to what the Bible says about God's continuing—but not endless—battle for the salvation of his creatures. Paul quotes Isaiah 65:2, "All day long I have held out my hands to a disobedient and obstinate people" (Romans 10: 21) indicating that all is in order now nor that all things go according to God's will and plan. It is not a verbal charade to pray that the will of God be "done on earth," where it is not yet being done, "as in heaven," where it is already being done. That is what Jesus taught us to pray, and I assume he saw the reality in history for what it is. If it were in the moral and factual power of God to get the job done at any time, why is it not being done yet? Or if God's work for justice, wholeness—*Shalom*, if you will—*is* being done, why are we asked to seek it, to pray, to be compassionate, and to resist evil? Why all the commands throughout the Bible if God could arrange the world and destroy what does not work, the way the potter would with clay, only to start again?

Some attempts to answer those questions are found in what is called the "Openness of God" view. It seeks to be more allied to our human experience, but makes similarly severe mistakes in neglecting what the Bible tells us. While Greek thought and modern mechanistic and deterministic hopes influenced later followers of Calvinism and their choice of verses to support their cause, "Openness of God" has focused on its own selection of passages and is largely influenced by postmodern desires for a God-at-hand, a personal relationship in which I can share my troubles with a friend who can hold my hand, support me, "and together we will manage it."

We shall come back to this curious proposition further on. But first we must look at another place where "predestination" refers to something quite different from what is today associated with Calvin, election, and determinism.

The God of the Bible is innocent of the kind of pushing about of Esau or Pharaoh for his ends, or of treating people like pots and pans in the messy kitchen of life. Such behavior, when attributed to the God of the Bible, would make him the responsible one behind Hitler and Stalin as well. Not only those mighty and evil people would be pawns in God's now-horrible work, but little folk as well. The shooting of classmates and teachers in Colorado, the nurse practicing euthanasia in Holland, the drunken driver that is used by God to get Uncle George to the funeral of the child run over—where, upon hearing a sermon, George believes: they all present a God who is guilty of history, when the Bible clearly states his innocence of evil. According to the Bible there are quite a number of additional participants in history, so that it is not at present going the right way.

CHAPTER SIX

REAL LIFE VERSUS
SPIRITUAL ESCAPE

Human Struggle or God's Effort?

The first chapter of Paul's letter to the church in Ephesus is another place where the word "predestined" occurs. The whole chapter revolves around God's choice to offer us salvation and much more. The letter was written in part against the Gnostic heresies that promoted, under the influence of Platonic ideas, a search for spiritual accomplishments by freeing oneself from matter, history, and reality by means of secret knowledge. The quest for this arcane knowledge, it was said, would achieve spiritual results and greater independence from a painful material existence.

Paul's response to these ideas is that we have in Christ the Godhead in bodily form (Colossians 2:9). Our God did not dwell in some remote galaxy but had come in the flesh. He is the creator of the material world; he came for lunch and discussions in it. We should not pursue the kind of spirituality that abstracts us from real life, from our bodies, from thought and reflection, or from the efforts to resist the results of the fall in a broken world through work, love, and creativity. The "Spiritual," Paul taught, is what God has communicated by means of his Spirit in word and work to tell us what he had had in mind when he made us in the first place. It informs our spirit so that we can live more truly and fully as human beings in the completeness of our being, both body and soul.

From God's Spirit, the author of the prophetic text, we know that we are not meant to be angels or wisps of ectoplasm. Neither are we to take life's experiences uncritically, just lying low. The word from God tells us from outside our visual reality how to look at all of life from the vantage point of God. This perspective not only tells us what is, but also what ought to be. We learn where it is no longer or not yet again and what we should do to bring it about.

In Ephesians Paul speaks of the spiritual accomplishments God has already gained for us. We have already received all spiritual blessings in Christ in heavenly places (1:3). We do not need secret knowledge, the denial of matter, or the abrogation of real life. We are not looking for ways to free the soul from the body or other ways to become spiritual. In Christ we have all the spiritual blessings we will ever need. Why?

In answer to this existential question Paul details the biblical view in one long sentence: in Christ we have been chosen to be holy and blameless (v. 4); through him (Christ) we have been predestined for adoption (v. 5); in the beloved (Christ) we have been blessed with glorious grace (v. 6); in him (Christ) we have redemption and forgiveness (v. 7); God lavished the riches of his grace on us, making known to us the mystery of his will and purpose, which he set forth in Christ (v. 8, 9). Another sentence continues: we, the Jews, have received an inheritance in him (Christ) (v. 11), according to his predestined purpose, and you also, the Gentiles, when you believed, were sealed with the Holy Spirit (v. 13) as a guarantee of our inheritance until we receive the full possession (v. 14).

And then it is all summed up for the present reality in verses 15 though 23. Ephesians' focal point is to restrain those who taught that humanity had to become in some way divine, reaching beyond the material world and history to achieve spiritual benefits and status. Jesus Christ trumps these aspirations. In Christ we have whatever humanity will ever seek, need, or desire, if we're honest with ourselves. Christ is the unique redeemer, the fountain of hope for the resurrection, the advocate with the Father. In him we know that God loves us. If he forgave us our sins, who can possibly accuse us? And before whom, in what court of law on earth or in heaven could such an accusation stand? For it is Christ who died, was raised and intercedes for us (Romans 8:34).

The subject matter in Ephesians chapters one and two is the total sufficiency of Christ. All the benefits we receive from God now and forever are because of Christ. There is nothing about our personal and individual predestination in that text. Every sentence sheds light on what God has done for us in Christ, the beloved, the revealed mystery, the redeemer, the signer of the adoption document with his own blood. We have not been chosen personally, but in Christ we were chosen to become blameless and again acceptable to God. In Christ God manifests what he has in mind for his creation and each of us. He is the express image of the father.

Only people seeking a special, "Gnostic," private affirmation would read this text as indicating something God has done for them and not for others. There is no exclusivity to God's gift in Christ to a particular person, though each person individually needs to accept this gift, one at a time. It is not exclusive in the sense that some are excluded from the possibility of having this acceptable gift presented to them.

Of course, that question of exclusivity touches on a central question in people's minds. Is God's knowledge the result of a selective process on the part of God, or does everyone stand before the need to seek after, find, and believe God? One will have to start with evidence of God's will, expressed in Scripture and in history. God ran after Adam to deal with the new situation that resulted from the fall. Ever since that scene in the ancient garden, the Bible portrays a God who grieves over sin, pleads with people to believe, and reveals his truth in the context of verifiable history, science, and reasonable evidence. God speaks through prophets and apostles, giving his word in the living Word. He sent a text through his Spirit (2 Peter 1:21) and reminds us of its content and comfort by the same Holy Spirit.

But when God has such a desire to be known, to be believed, and to be loved, why do people not become believers and show it by obedience to his character? In the controlled situations assumed by fatalism, mechanism, and a theology of total divine control, the only answer can be that God does not want them to believe. When the system is closed, there is no open-ended history, no personality, and no choice.

What, in Fact, is Wrong (With Us)?

It is curious how a double set of assumptions from a flawed reading of Scripture can lead to such a terrible view of God and humanity. Rather than answering the questions of our age, this warped perception confirms the worst fears and reactions to Christianity in our generation. Why does so much of the Church plunk itself right into the middle of this error with its teaching of selective manipulation from God, thereby provoking people's furious reactions and careless excuses? Why do we refuse to proclaim instead the surprising, wholesome, and living truth of the Bible?

It is more than curious—it is maddening. In contrast to the Christ who reached out to people, the Church is often like the Pharisees who restrain people from knowing God by speaking of moral and factual absurdities.

The god of the "selective church" is a deity who really does not want people to know him and who, therefore, makes it impossible. This god does not make additional efforts to explain and examine reality in what is now the normal world by revealing its abnormality when compared to creation in the past before the fall and to resurrection in the future. This examination would be required to understand the perversity of the present as man's, not God's, responsibility. God, as the near-sighted present him, hides in his holiness, speaks about a world unknown, and makes himself seem totally unrelated, absurd, and incomprehensible. The common man has no access to this god. Only the religious freak, the village idiot, or the man in pursuit of his own mysteries is attracted to this version of the spiritual life.

Yet many Christians arrive at these stunted conclusions one way or another, either when they hold that humankind is so sinful that are unable to seek after God or when they are totally disinterested in knowing anything about God. In their reading, the fall of Adam became a total separation; God has turned his back on us. There is nothing good anymore in the human race, therefore God rejects us. The above view of predestination underscores that there is nothing humanity can do to find out about God and the ways of God.

The Bible shows the heinousness of sin. "Be ye holy, even as I am holy" is a standard none of us can reach. "The wages of sin are death" follows the warning of God to Adam, that the day he eats of the forbidden fruit he shall die. Sin destroys not just beauty, but all perfection, and renders it unacceptable. This is confirmed by the work of Christ in that he bore our sins in his own body on the cross and was consequently forsaken by the Father until his work was finished. Before God, no sin or imperfection is acceptable.

In addition to this "sinful nature," our "being dead spiritually" and the declaration that "there is no one righteous, not even one; there is no one who understands, no one who seeks God" (Romans 3:10–11) contributed to our sensible understanding of the total depravity of humanity. It is indeed hopeless, for all the good in the world cannot erase the problems we carry with us from the past.

Yet again we need to look at these and related concepts from Ephesians in light of the whole of Scripture to cleanse spiritual insight from cultural poison added in some theological kitchen. How did such a term as "total depravity" arise? What could color our understanding of Romans 3:12? How does a cultural context contribute an unhelpful subtext to our reading of the text? How does this affect (or infect) our "reading" of human nature or being dead in sin?

Starting with the concept of "total depravity" as it was originally intended, we can see by its connotation that in no area of our thought and material life are we perfect. We are born from and into an imperfect world, marked in all areas by the results of the fall. The "totality" expanded across all human efforts, skills and accomplishments. In no area of our lives can we point to perfection.

In addition, it is clear that when perfection is marred it has become imperfection. A "second" purchased at a factory outlet is imperfect, even when it is still able to hold water or to be worn under a jacket. For the same reason James reminds us that "whoever keeps the whole law and yet stumbles at just one point is guilty of breaking all of it" (2:10). This does not suggest that we are guilty of breaking all laws, but rather that we no longer have the glory of perfection. We are all imperfect across the board and in all parts.

This universal imperfection should have been admitted when the Roman church gave the impression from its teaching that one could bargain with God in one area or another to receive grace from God. "Sainthood" or the brotherhood of the saints in the Roman church no longer included every believer in Christ, even though Paul called all the believers in Corinth "saints of Jesus Christ" (see 1 Corinthians 1:2) with all their confused, mixed-up, and often very sinful ways and views, which he addressed in his letter to them. Instead, for Rome a saint was someone who had reached perfection and had been accepted by God into heaven on that merit. Proof of this was established when they performed miracles or when their bodies did not decompose.

We must admit that we do fall short of the God's glory. We are not what we were intended to be as Adam's children in a good world. We have damaged minds and broken bodies. But we are not totally depraved, or corrupt through and through, or good for nothing. That is not the picture Jesus gives of all those citizens in normal work who appear in his parables. He never accuses his neighbor of total depravity. Paul does not have people's ontological perversity in mind when he admonished the church in Thessalonica to work for their living so that their daily life may win the respect of outsiders (1 Thessalonians 4:12), or when he says that we should devote ourselves to doing what is good and not live unproductive lives (Titus 3:14). There are many passages in the Old and New Testament where people are praised and where good work is honored.

Noah is called a "righteous man" and is singled out with his family to survive the flood in an ark. He believed God's warning and started building that enormous ship before it ever started to rain. We can imagine how the people laughed at him. "What a foolish man," they said, "on dry land to go sailing," are the words of a wonderful chorus. But that is not the faith that mattered to God primarily. Neither is there any indication that Noah is called righteous only because he believed in the promise to Abraham about the coming Savior. Instead, Genesis 6:9 tells us that, "Noah was righteous, because he was blameless among the people of his time and he walked with God." He did not behave the way others around him did. He was not perfect, for no one is after the fall. But that did not make him totally depraved. He was a righteous man. What affirmation, what credit to his choices, what remarkable courage to walk with God rather than to join the crowd!

God's Image in Human Faces

Being imperfect in all areas is not the same as being depraved throughout. Men and women, widows and orphans, well or ill, humanity never loses the image of God. We are never junk. Sin never destroys the reflection of God in human faces (see Genesis 9:6). We need renewal, restoration, and the resurrection to be made perfect again. That is the standard acceptable to God. But anything short of that is not total depravity, except in the area of moral innocence. The "totality" people spoke about in the seventeenth century was a measure of width across all areas of life, not of depth.

Even Romans 3:12 does not teach what is often read into it in many circles. It does not give us a definition of humanity the way one would make a classification in biology, state a legal definition in court, or a describe an attribute in theology. Man is not by his nature, the way he now is or had been made by God, one who "is not righteous, does not seek, does not understand." In fact he is by nature a seeking being. Curiosity is a human characteristic. We transcend the mere present through questions, thought, and investigation. All science and art are expressions of this need for us to know more than our present experience.

Humans alone inquire about life beyond the surface of things. We seek after God and look for meaning behind events. Our searching is very often not according to truth. We abandon reason and reality easily. Facts are frequently left out of our equations. We will make gods in our image all too readily and do the kind of things Paul describes in Romans 1:21 and following. But it cannot be said that we do not seek, never understanding. If that were so, a multitude of other statements about the divine-human dance would have to be obliterated. They would no longer fit a comprehensive reading of Scripture.

Scripture assumes that we *do* seek, even though often at the wrong place and with a dishonest heart and mind. For this reason we frequently find God promising that "if you seek the Lord your

God you will find him, if you look for him with all your heart and with all your soul" (Deuteronomy 4:29).

But of course a simplistic reading of Romans 3:12 would possibly explain why the Joe next door does not believe what I believe. Such verses give a comfort of sorts about the puzzle each person is to the other, but they do not do justice to Joe or to the God who desires to bring Joe to knowledge of God, life, and salvation. Such readings do a disservice because there are Joes in life who seek to know the truth and find it in bits and pieces. The difference between various people is more related to their honesty and integrity about the real world, real people, and real questions than some belief that people are ontologically cast from an identical mold, dead to righteousness, seeking, and understanding.

What Real Excuse Do We Have?

Instead let us look at the passage. It stands in the flow of Paul's argument that we are all under God's wrath, because we are each guilty for our willful denial of what is true. We profess ourselves to be wise, when in fact we are fools in our interpretation of reality (Romans 1:18–22). Only God's word gives the fitting key for an accurate interpretation. The Greek cannot say that he did not know God's laws, for he is condemned on the basis of not keeping his own relative standards. The Jew cannot appeal to his personal and special relationship to God, for he does not keep the laws he received as part of the Covenant.

Both Greek and Jew are in the same mess. Neither one of them is better than the other. Both are charged with being under sin (Romans 3:9). Neither is acceptable to God where they have arrived in their faiths. Not one or the other understands what is true in the universe. Neither of them have sought God in their situation of alienation under God's wrath. These are the words Paul used in Romans 3:11. He quotes them from Psalms, which report the words of "the fool (who) says in his heart, 'there is no

God'" (Psalm 14:1–3; Psalm 53:1–3). He could also have quoted Ecclesiastes 7:20, "There is not a righteous man on earth who does what is right and never sins," or from Isaiah 59:7, "Their feet rush into sin; they are swift to shed innocent blood. Their thoughts are evil thoughts; ruin and destruction mark their ways."

This lament over human wickedness and foolishness expresses God's sorrow that neither Gentile nor Jew does much about their situation. It is not a legal definition of humanity in general. "There is none, no not one . . ." refers to Gentile and Jew, who are addressed until now in Paul's letter to the church in Rome. It cannot mean that there is no single seeker anywhere in the universe. Both Gentiles and Jews need salvation and are brought together in the one sacrifice of Christ, just as in chapter four which explains both believers before Christ's death and those after it are brought together in the common hope we have in the Messiah.

It must mean this, for in the preceding chapters the accusation against them (and each of us) is precisely that they should have sought but did not. That is why we are "without excuse" (Romans 1:20). It is not a case of people not being able to seek until God awakens them to spiritual hunger. Paul says that we knew what can be known of God, it is plain to us (1:19), things have been clearly revealed to us, and we have perceived them (1:20). Yet we suppressed the truth in unrighteousness (1:18), we hold it under our thumb, we hide it under our hats. Against better evidence from the created reality around us, we made a lousy judgment to believe something that makes no sense.

I think Paul would have argued in our context something like this: You realize that we live in an ordered universe, and yet you choose to believe in chance, even though nowhere do you have evidence of real randomness. How stupid! You know how different human beings are from everything else. We speak, animals make noise and signal. We praise and blame others as if they had a choice in their actions, yet we say we believe we are just a more complicated animal who follows social and material conditioning or that impersonal matter lies at the origin of personal beings. We assert that a closed system can bring forth open choices. How foolish, how inconsistent, how unreal! How do you expect to get away with that and remain credible?

In other words we have is a capacity to know, to choose; to accept or reject. We act foolishly when we believe contrary to the evidence. The whole tenor of Scripture is to address our minds, to urge us to reflect, compare and decide what we are going to believe about anything. Sin has separated us from pure knowledge. We are now outside the Garden of Eden. But God has run after us, sent letters by prophets and apostles and dwelt among us in his Son from heaven. While the Son returned to heaven, God has given us his Spirit so that we would be reminded that what Scripture speaks is true. The apostles reasoned, preached, expounded, exhorted, argued, and set forth again and again the truth, and many people responded with understanding and belief. The evidence was clearly argued, and some of the listeners chose to acknowledge it and draw their beneficial conclusions.

The earliest Church did not understand texts and concepts like being "dead in sin" or "spiritually dead" to mean what some now suggest it to mean. Such "death" is not indicative of an incapacity to live, to choose, and to seek. The image or concept of being "dead" here cannot be extended to mean lifeless, no heartbeat, no brain activity. "Dead in sin" (Ephesians 2:1) stands in relation to judgment, not existence. It is legal, not existential. There has been a moral death, not an execution. We are alive as human beings with all our curiosity, creativity, and longing. Certainly being "dead in sin" would not deny that the person is able to actively sin, be clever about it and happy to get away with it. A sinner can also be kind to his neighbor, diagnose an illness well, and refine a complicated procedure. He can lead an active life in pursuit of his values, as we like to say in our generation.

We are also not "dead" in efforts to make sense out of reality. We are able to weigh propositions and seek wisdom. Doing this for reasons of personal survival or for understanding of where we have come from and what it all means is not an indication of spiritual death. Children, women, and men, artists and philosophers have tried to raise such questions. The spiritual death the Bible speaks about does not describe an inability to seek, but rather a choice to limit the areas in which I admit answers. Spiritual death results from dishonesty. It does not furnish a definition of humanity separated from the image of God.

The result of sin is death, the results of believing what is not factual is being foolish. Believing that I can live in a world other than God's world will lead first to spiritual death (an absence from God's fellowship and love) and then also to physical death (when I don't respect the laws of nature designed by the creator). But even this truth does not mean that I will cease to exist as a conscious person.

Being "dead in sin" cannot mean that one is incapable of doing anything, as if one's physical body were dead. Why, even the devil knows and trembles! He is very much alive, yet spiritually dead. Adam was told that disobedience would lead to death. There was an immediate part and a later part, but no final death. His legal status would change immediately, later his physical body would return to dust in death. But at no time was he or will he ever be gone, dissolved, annihilated and no longer bear the image of God. Being "spiritually dead" after the fall describes a moral and legal situation; this does not prevent God from coming and speaking to Adam. Neither does it incapacitate Adam from hearing and responding to God. God did not have to make Adam alive after he disobeyed and ate; he was never dead. Nor did God make him spiritually alive. The Bible merely says that God talked to him. Adam wa//s guilty and in need of forgiveness through the coming Messiah. For this God killed an animal to cover their legal problem. Nonetheless, Adam was neither unable to respond nor disinterested in what he heard.

The Spiritual Explains the Factual

Another way to look at it is to see how the word "spiritual" is used in similar contexts. Paul says that spiritual truth needs to be discerned spiritually (1 Corinthians 2:14). But he has already explained in this context that if the Greek listeners sought wisdom in the contemplation of their own ideals of beauty, rhetoric, and justice and therefore found the word of the cross foolish (1:18), our wisdom is not of another kind, as if it were ugly, dumb, and irrational. The difference lies in the fact that it originated from another author with another content, which the Greeks would not accept. God's Spirit tells us what is in God's mind. We understand something spiritually when we have understood what the Holy Spirit has explained about how things really are.

"Spiritual" in the Bible does not indicate something in opposition to material, nor to what is rational, creational, or moral. The Russian Orthodox view of seeing a higher spiritual awareness in the poor, the sick, and the unthinkingly submissive shows the influence of Plato where Jesus should have a say instead. Likewise, "spiritually dead" is the person who does not have what the Holy Spirit was given to bring to believers after Christ ascended to his father's house. They don't have the reality and experience of adoption certainty, of sonship, comfort, truth, and advocacy before God. But it says nothing of an inability to seek God or an absence of desire to know who God is.

When you see more than this in "spiritual death," you have turned the human being into something that fits into your system of divine selection. You will have confused the inability to merit grace with an inability to seek the grace of God. Such hyper-sensitivity (and its attendant introspection) makes one afraid that seeking (or wishing to believe a credible and living God) itself could be construed as a merit. Instead you would prefer to see the fallen humanity's remaining glory in being human put to death than acknowledge a merciful God who chose to offer redemption even to those who reject it for their own reasons, therefore having no excuse that they were not among the elect.

The great fear in some circles is that something of value to God remains in humanity after the fall with which humans might bargain with God or claim salvation. That is an understandable concern, for any bargaining chip diminishes the total distance between sinful people and a holy God. Yet the human search to understand and find answers is not a "work" that counts toward merit. Why is the discussion limited to an either/or between two extreme options, rather than seeing that humanity is valuable to God for reasons of having been created by him. The Bible declares a God who does not abandon his creation but runs after it to redeem it.

The theological fear of sounding like people can make an effort to earn the merit of Christ (an apprehension made tangible in Roman Catholic theology for a long time before and after the Reformation) is understandable. One is not limited to an option, though, in which God becomes in some form dependent on human effort to accomplish salvation. Neither is the common alternative of this view found in Scripture. Nothing in the Bible states that God has chosen you personally, set you apart from many others, in order that you might believe, while others can't believe until they are similarly set apart.

That view expresses perhaps more the experiential joy of the believer than biblical theology. It rightly emphasizes the personal interest of God in our salvation. It reminds us of the full price God is prepared to pay for our forgiveness and resurrection, when we had nothing with which to weigh in. It brings out the marvelous work of God on our behalf, without which there would be no salvation.

But all these wonderful points can be justly maintained without having to turn salvation into a personal mystery, an experience of God's selection of a dead piece of wood or a potter's vessel, which he then regenerates and turns into a believing human being.

"From the beginning God chose you to be saved through the sanctifying work of the Spirit and through belief in the truth. He called you to this through our gospel, that you might share in the glory of our Lord Jesus Christ" (2 Thessalonians 2:13–14). This passage speaks of the whole work of God through each member of the Trinity, forming the "locus" of our wonder, awe, and thankfulness. The work of the Spirit will sanctify your salvation to obtain the glory of Jesus Christ. It says nothing about regeneration being required to enable a person to believe. Only a culture in love with either personal destiny (as found in pre-scientific superstition) or personal rights and advantages (found in democratic individualism) will focus on the chosen and immediate self instead of God.

Paul says in Romans 8:7 that "the sinful mind is hostile to God" without stating that there is a necessity of maintaining such carnality. The princes and wise folk of this world did not recognize Christ, because they delighted, as did the Greeks of 1 Corinthians 1:18–25, in their own course, thought world and beliefs. The path of the sinful has nothing to do with God having elected other people elsewhere. "You will seek me and find me when you seek me with all your heart" (Jeremiah 29:13).

Guilty From Folly and Indifference

In my experience, many reject God and his mercy in response to a distorted caricature of Christianity characterized by this low view about human beings. If there is a spirit of the age that blinds us today, it is also found in the Greek view of God wherever it is held by the Church in distinction to the Jewish/biblical one. People reject what they hear presented as Christianity though they have never heard biblical responses to their questions. Christians believe they give scripturally grounded answers, but their answers often leave God first guilty of manipulation and then indifferent to a messy world reputedly of his design and making to begin with. That proposition is morally reprehensible and intellectually more of what all religions teach already, only now with different names and peculiar practices.

The unique difference of Christianity, of God, men, and women in history took Paul two years to explain in Ephesus, while many of us believe that communicating the Christian gospel can be done today with a tract. We are irresponsibly shallow when we assume that the Church deserves a hearing when we do not cover content as similar and complete as what Paul taught during his two weeks in Thessalonica. He gave more than a few spiritual laws or an invitation to love, hope, and faith. When he referred to these Christian realities, he fleshed them out with a larger content. Love, hope, and faith are the result of Paul having laid out a completely different worldview from anything the Greek citizens in town had ever heard. There was no fate anymore, no cycle to life, no confusion among the gods, and a moral judgment at the end of linear history (See 1 Thessalonians 1:9–10).

Paul also taught biblical ethics about marriage, respect for human beings, social engagement, and work, and he concludes with a biblical approach to life and death (ch. 4). He urged the believers to be more alert, critical, and discerning of their culture.

As a result of such content, the whole world was eventually changed, beginning in the Roman Empire. With Christianity, Europe became a separate continent of ideas and practices, much more than only geographically, and then spread them across the world.

Such wealth and beauty, such intellectual answers and social realities we, however, have abandoned in what has become our central interest: personal relations, feeling better, and drawing more elect people into our support group.

Our human nature is precisely never, in the way God treats us, destroyed. We have a profound legal and a creational problem because of Adam's sin and ours. But we never cease being human beings who can and must think, seek, and discover. Only from foolishness do we believe what is wrong, only from selected evidence do we come to faulty conclusions. Evidence may be withheld deliberately; truth may be distorted. Surrounding culture and religious teaching may seek to cover up or distort the evidence of reality. Yet reality demands a verdict which most religions do not provide. They tend to deny parts of that reality. Wherever reality is admitted, the shoe of religion will be too small for my feet and pinch.

I must then take it off to wiggle my toes in greater freedom until I find a shoe that fits. And there the Bible gives such comfort, such encouragement, such an affirmation to the human being with God's promise that "whoever seeks me with his whole heart shall surely find me," a truth said in various ways throughout Scripture. The jailor in Philippi, Nicodemus by night, Martin Luther reading the Bible—anyone really seeking—God will find him. Finding God is not a matter of accomplishing something, but of God's promise that he will reveal himself to us. God ties himself down to do what it takes to become known by us. On the individual level only a lack of honesty, not a designation as spiritually dead, will stand in the way of genuine discovery.

Our barber at the beginning of the book has only ever looked at real life, history, and most of the Church's teaching. These sources do not reveal God's mind, desire, and actions. He has never looked at the Bible, that Word which speaks not through reality, but about it. It judges reality, encourages revolt and asks to be taken as a whole. "Man does not live on bread alone but on every word that comes from the mouth of the Lord" (Deuteronomy 8:3).

It is clear that we cannot save ourselves. It is too late for that; we are already damaged, imperfect, and morally guilty. We have nothing we can bargain with. We rightly reject any notion of "works" contributing to fill the measure of God's requirement to "be holy, even as (he is) holy." Yet the fear among some Protestants to mention works, effort, human and professional qualities has led us to embrace a very distorted image of humanity that is not biblical any longer. God never treats fallen humanity as unworthy of his love, grace, and effort. "For it is by grace you have been saved, through faith—and this not from yourselves, it is the gift of God—not by works, so that no one can boast" (Ephesians 2:8–9).

This "grace" is what Paul has been building up to all along. It is Christ, the gift of God for our salvation, unmerited, freely given. "Grace" is not an act of God to select some to salvation, but the gift of God, an unmerited favor, which he presents to the world in the finished work of Christ. God has predestined all kinds of realities mentioned in the first chapter of Ephesians and accomplished them through Christ's sacrifice for us.

God is not shopping for souls in a messy world. He is not choosing some and rejecting others. What God has done for us in Christ Jesus is to present us with a gift, which, like any gift ever, needs to be accepted. We do that by faith, which means that we conclude that God is not lying about it. We can freely believe him and be thankful. The gift is Christ. There is no deceit or disappointment about that gift. He is God and judge. Christ takes away the moral guilt of those who believe him to do this in his death and resurrection. We check it out and find that it is reasonable, true to the promises, historic and powerful, for Jesus was raised from the dead, the first of many.

Believing this to be true and relying on its content is faith, through which we declare our thankfulness, wonder, and dedication. Faith is not the gift spoken of here in Ephesians 2:8–9, how human beings always respond to evidence, real or imaginary. Faith is part of being human, the ability to conclude that there is enough evidence to rely on. The scientist believes with the evidence of his experiences. The lover believes the observations he has made and what she knows about the loved one. "Faith is the assurance of things hoped for (on the basis of good evidence), the conviction of things not (exhaustively) seen" (Hebrews 11:1 NASB, with author notes). Any medical doctor functions this way when he believes the complaints of his patients, uses his diagnostic skills and proposes a treatment. He has to believe it first to practice medicine. In fact faith is the way we know anything.

Before God, faith has no bartering value. Faith does not constrain God to action and is not a condition for God to give salvation. But faith is a condition without which we cannot receive anything, neither medical help nor salvation in Christ.

God never treats humanity as incapable of seeking or free from responsibility for failing to seek. "Come now and let us reason together," or, "Should you inquire of the dead on behalf of the living," are part of a list of such efforts to make himself be known. These are honest questions on the part of God to us. Jesus sought the crowds to address them. The Apostles spoke at length to the mind and heart of listeners wherever they found them. Amos the prophet was sent to the hostile Northern Kingdom to speak to the authorities, much to their annoyance. Elijah warned Ahab of the judgment to come (1 Kings 17). Jonah preached in Nineveh, and most of the inhabitants of that great city repented.

When the Bible speaks of the basic problem of humanity in terms of its foolish beliefs and its rejection of God, it points out the need for turning around to the greater evidence of God, to greater faithfulness to reason and the real world, to the Word and instructions of the Creator. It does not speak of an impossibility of humanity to think, to make choices and to change ways. *Our* sin is not part of *his* system. There is no flaw in our ability to know, only in our desire to be consistent with reality. And that desire is a matter of choice.

Therefore we are not in a closed system. We do not have a destiny that dictates events. There is no fate controlling all of life. Our situation is not totally constraining. We live in a context of reality, in which past choices have produced inevitable consequences. But we also live in a reality in which people can create alternatives, invent new ways, get on top of circumstances, and repent. We are not completely caught in a chain of cause and effect. Christianity and Judaism do not produce cultures and attitudes of endless chains of "again and again."

God is innocent of what people have done or continue to do every day. He is Lord, but not a sovereign puppeteer. The God of the Bible is not "in control" in any kind of deterministic understanding. The God of the Bible is not a mechanism. He treats people the way he made them to act: by choice, creatively and responsibly.

During my lectures for many years in the former Soviet Union, I kept pointing out how our Christian view of men and women in the West excludes any final determinism behind human existence. There is a form to reality, but within that form people are able to create, choose, and act. The stars do not determine behavior. A choice is different from matter functioning on matter.

All their lives, Russians have heard the opposite: history determines events, energy functions mechanistically in their lives, the party determines what people do and how they live. But in God we have an awakened independence and responsibility to create history, rather than to suffer as a part of it. Evil must be resisted, a more balanced diet and exercise implemented, better medication and technologies found, relationships formed from love and respect. There is no total inevitability for man, and only the Bible explains why and how.

How tragic that many Christians do not understand these various links but introduce God with characteristics very similar to those of the older Fates. Instead of state and history, is it now supposed to be God controlling their lives? But they have lived under control all their lives! The creativity and individual responsibility has been beaten out of them. They wait, as on the sidelines of life, until things happen; and evil people will make things happen! When the demon is driven out and not replaced with the Spirit of God, the demon and all his seven friends will return.

God is not in this kind of control. Sin reigns where it was chosen. There is a war going on, and we take sides in it. We avoid being swallowed up along the way by "test[ing] everything that is said. Hold on to what is good" (1 Thessalonians 5:21 NLT). Then we can have a say in history by the choices people make, the communities they create, and in policies they pursue. What a horror to the human spirit to leave him only with a Christian version of the same determined flow of events which controls all reality and allows for no human contribution.

CHAPTER SEVEN

INFINITE-PERSONAL GOD
AND
FINITE-PERSONAL HUMAN

The central question remains: is God guilty or innocent? We need to address it further. Is God almighty (*El-Shaddai*) and in control? If he is in control, is he good *and* evil, and are we mistaken when we see these as opposites? Or has God died?

As we consider this more closely we need to make a small excursion in our minds to consider alternatives as well as implications of what the Bible tells us. Doing this has led to wonderful results in people's hearts, minds, and lives. When they read the Bible, they realized that God made us with a purpose, that he loves us, and that we are meant to be people. As people, we were not to take our cues about life from circumstances, but from God. We would understand things better because we could think, which was necessary if we are to understand God's Word rather than merely being exposed to creation as our neighborhood. We can observe in the Word, the Bible, and God's actions that creation is quite a mess now. God is not at home here, and he is not at all pleased.

The God of the Bible is stated to be someone specific. He is not everything existing, assuming of course that you, me, and the text under your eyes exist. God is someone who thinks, feels, and acts. More than that, there is a plurality or diversity in the Godhead forever. For they decide to create together: "Let us make" reflects this plurality. Kings and presidents of nations other than the Jews used such a formulation as a plural of majesty in their speeches and letters. The Jews, however, never used it except to indicate several personages. King David never speaks of himself as "we." Jews were aware that elsewhere the plural of majesty was usual, but they did not employ it. A person's value, power, or esteem does not derive from his multiplying himself or being more formal or more important. The Bible presents God as Trinity of distinct persons. The Father loved the Son from before the foundation of the world.

God created a real world with increasing details and differentiations. He took time for that and gave the mandate to continue creation to humankind, male and female, equally in the image of God.

God looked at everything he had made and was pleased. It was all very fitting, or "good," a word that is derived from the word "god" and indicates that nothing was out of place, in disarray, ugly, or in conflict in the original creation. But it was all outside of God, distinct from him, though not out of his presence. God is never absent, uninvolved, or merely observing as the deists taught.

This is important for our discussion, for it means that there is a certain limitation to the eternal God. Creation did not make God bigger; it did not emanate from him. God is not the totality of what is. Creation was *vis-à-vis* to God. The infinite God of the Bible is not all-inclusive. There is a reality outside of God, for he brought it into being in its precise forms, or nature, outside himself.

There is also a second limitation to the God of the Bible. He is infinite in his personality, his character. This means two things. Infinity is a kind of measure. It addresses quantities, while personality is a matter of definition and qualities. Practically it tells us that God's characteristic love is not confused with hate, his patience is not indifference, his mercy is not judgmental. He is infinite in who he is, but he is not infinity as such. One can also say it this way: the practice of his attributes never comes to an end. There is an infinitely inexhaustible measure of his specific love, but it is never confused with hate. Consequently, some real things are excluded from God or outside him. They only exist outside and in distinction of or even in opposition to God. For instance, there is no deceit in God, no evil, no death. These are creations of later creatures, both among angels and men, and not part of the eternal God of the Bible.

God is then in a real way, and not just in terms of language, limited to being a particular God with certain attributes. We will see more implications of this in the next chapter. Here I want to draw attention to the fact that attributes are qualifiers to God, like adjectives to a noun. They do not define or limit God to have a specific character and personality, as if someone else imposed them from outside or behind God. It is rather that such clarifying adjectives of God's attributes, his being and personality, are writ large and loud in bold affirmations and distinctives. Our God is not unknowable. Words do not slide past him. He is the living Word, and because of this he can talk, communicate, and make his will known. One cannot speak of God as personality or mind with all that this communicates and at the same time assume that God is just infinite. Infinity cannot even be expressed, since every word defines a particular slice of reality.

We have then in the Bible a specific God who exists forever and whose being is forever faithful. This affirmation of the person of God, his eternal existence, does not mean that everything is already and forever "now" to him. His knowledge of all things does not imply his experience of all things co-equally or even at any time. Therefore he knows what a unicorn would look like, but he never made one. He chose to create a world without unicorns, but with a platypus, eels, and other fierce and unusual creatures.

For a second reason there is no need to place all reality into an "Eternal Now" before God. There was a "before" creation, followed by an "after" creation; "before" Christ's finished work and "after;" a "not yet" about the coming of the Holy Spirit and "then" an outpouring on Pentecost. Michelangelo's painting of "The Creation of Adam" in Rome shows that God had Eve in mind when he made Adam. She is there among the angels in the other arm of God. But she did not come into existence until after Adam had first been made with bones. Then Eve was made as Adam's helpmeet.

We see that the Bible does not present a God who is simply infinite in contrast to our finiteness, but there is more. God created a real world but then told the human beings to create realities God could not have created. I imagine, though I am not directly told, that Adam and Eve were created as adults, not babies. They were then in turn to have babies just like apple trees were made to produce apples. Adam and Eve were created as adults, since babies depend on parents and only the next generation could have Adam and Eve as parents. Having babies and growing apples is part of the nature of creation, but not in the nature of God. God made things and people to function in certain ways and thereby to increase what he had first made out of nothing. A stage is set with props and definitions, but it is up to the actors to accept the encouragement of the director to fill the world with words and actions and to use props.

Natural things function according to their template, which means they cannot do anything else. They repeat what their instructions tell them. They follow the laws typical of their nature. But the typical nature of human beings is to be persons, i.e., to think, to love, to imagine, to invent. Our bodies conform to their nature. Our minds in their nature need instruction from outside to know what is wise and good, especially since, in a fallen world, we don't know from inside ourselves what our purpose is, nor what is good. All kinds of actions are now typical of human beings around us, and a broken universe with life and death no longer models goodness, peace, or harmony in any clear form.

The creator instructs us by means of language, sentences, and concepts. He explains purposes, relationships, and inquiry to our minds. He expects us to reason with those propositions and to discover their quality. Discernment is a constant admonition in Scripture precisely because we must choose and then face the consequences.

Having both God and Man, male and female "in the image of God," describes a situation in which there are many players on the stage of life. (We deliberately leave out the angels and their choices, though they also figure in creation.) My point is that in real history we have acts of God. And we have original acts of human beings that are not controlled, or in any way caused, by God. He trains us by instruction, not by behavior modification through stimulus and response, nor by our genetic constitution. He appeals to our minds and enjoys the good consequences of our creativity. We add to what God has made, even when we create things that are a lie. That's what happened at the Fall.

Adam and Eve created a fallen world, where death would slowly cover everything like a fine and poisonous dust. This was not God's plan, neither his desire. He had tried to prevent that with words, with warnings, and with a good world. Yet it was within the shape of a creation with personages that reality would never be static, history would never be repetitive, and tomorrow would be different from today. The creature made history within the bounds of what God had made. God acts into that history to restore it, augment it, redirect it, and simultaneously with the creature doing what is within his nature: to create.

It is not all part of the original master plan. Creation is a framework of conditions and definitions. It is not the cause of human action, but rather it defines the playing field on which human actions take place. There is no final cause for them other than that it lies within the "image-of-the-creator" to originate choices.

We have a God who is sad, furious, active, and troubled, but also capable of doing that extra work that is required to bring in "everlasting righteousness" (Daniel 9:24) again. Both God and the creatures as persons initiate choices and act into reality with consequences to each other. God does that within the boundaries of his character, the creature within the boundaries of being human. Whatever reason brought forth, any personal choice is not a prior cause or a determining condition, but the way persons think, act, and express themselves. For the same reason, by having a choice, we can also reject the best reasoning and act irrationally.

God knew all this ahead of time, of course. But his knowledge does not produce all events. Creative choices do that. God did not make Adam as sinful, but free to sovereignly, and from himself, choose to continue in the love in which and for which he had been made a human being, or to turn his back on it and to seek another direction. He could believe God or disbelieve him. His choice was for or against love, obedience, and fellowship. It was not a choice between good and evil. Only the choice to disbelieve God brought evil into existence in the human realm for the first time.

History of Interwoven Choices

The Bible clearly states that God did not in any way determine what Adam did. There was no causal relation between God's knowledge and the creature's choice. God's knowledge is truly infinite, but it does not cause an action in another person. God's knowledge does not in any compelling way, materially or intellectually, influence the creature's choice. In contrast to such notions, God pleads with man, argues with him, can even make donkeys talk to the obstinate, or changes the context of a person's reflection. God acts at all times into history. Yet there is no causal or necessary relationship between God's moral, ambitious, and passionate intervention and the free acts of real personages or agents. Actions express a deliberate choice to prefer, create and value a freely chosen original goal, idea, reality, or effort. Anything less than that makes God the cause by force, setup, or manipulation. None of these are evidenced in the Bible.

Neither do certain views about the decrees of God or what is called his foreordination of events correspond to what the Bible talks about. The influence of Greek thought and pagan fatalism must very carefully be kept out of Jewish biblical thought at all times. Much of the trouble in the discussion about God's responsibility for human evil or the state of the world starts here. In discussion the two can easily be confused. Greek and Hebraic views could not be further apart.

Greek and pagan views start with the idea that a transcendent and invisible power is in charge and controls all events. Transferred into Christian teaching, these views come out as God the Sovereign created our world, including for some unknown reason also sin and death. This view of God would cover all reality and sees a divine purpose behind all of it. At any moment the world is then always the best possible world. Yet this is not the biblical idea. God alone is Lord, but creatures also create significantly in history, including evil, which even God cannot ignore. That is why I mentioned God starting to work again on the eighth day. The sin of Adam changed the whole equation. God did not will or cause this change, nor could he have prevented it. But a new enterprise, an engagement toward redemption at a high price, is started. God runs after Adam and asks, "Where are you?" The promise of the Messiah and the rules for holiness and life are the mission and business plans in the mess Adam's sin created.

The decrees of God are the express determinations of God to get something done. First it was creation in its form, then the labor of interference and repair for our restoration after the fall. In addition, as Ed Veith[1] very helpfully points out, God works by means. He designed and created all natural processes. He also uses the means of his Word, his acts of grace, accessible language and dreams explained, and miraculous acts. He calls the church to exhibit spiritual care over his people. He uses natural laws, moral laws, and various callings or vocations in human life to bring about his purposes. He calls bakers to bake our bread, mechanics to fix our cars, and governments and their agents in the police, in courts, and in jails, even the military, to serve the good and to be agents of wrath to evildoers. God's providence refers to his care to provide for life in the chemistry of nature and the biology of our bodies, in nutrition and digestion.

God acts by all kinds of means. In that framework exist the specific actions chosen by Man. God's decrees and his providence include the fact that all human choices have rational, lawful, and consistent consequences. It is lawful for apple trees to produce apples. Psalm 104 runs through a long list of wise works of God (v. 24) in all creation, among them the sky, the sea and the mountains, the animals and plants, even the weather patterns.

But then the human response is one of song and praise, of thought and meditation, of desiring to be a pleasure to God and rejoicing in the Lord (v. 33–34). Our faith serves God, our works serve our neighbor and people in general, in an interaction of various callings. These actions are choices, not decrees of God. It is lawful for the inanimate creation to function according to their received program of being things. It is lawful for human beings to make free choices for which they alone are responsible.

---

1. Gene Edward Veith, Jr., *God at Work, Your Christian Vocation in All of Life* (Wheaton, IL: Crossway Books, 2002).

It is decreed that we live in a rational universe and not in a topsy-turvy one. You eat poisonous mushrooms and you will get very ill, if you even survive them, regardless of your religious convictions, personal intentions, nationality, gender, or sexual preference. This is a logical, lawful universe. There is no god, force or fate that will disturb the neatness of God's decrees that such a world exists. The notion that he has "ordained whatever comes to pass" refers to reality functioning lawfully. There will be justice, a reality of cause and effect, and lasting results from the work of Christ for all creation.

With the same rationality human beings will make choices. That is in our nature. What choices we make is a matter of personal decisions, selected priorities, and of love. Each choice will carry its own ordained consequence. In the world that God ordained, you will not be able to have your cake and eat it as well, nor are there free lunches or a grace that is free to God. God's creation and his Word demonstrate reasonable consequences to any choice. Reality speaks louder than any superstition and old wives tales against the experience of injustice as seemingly normal and lasting.

Human reality is not an experience of an inevitable chain of events ordained solely by the knowledge and will of God. It also includes wicked acts and crazy preferences by the will of Man, not to mention the works of the evil one. But God has ordained that there would be consequences to each choice, first real pain and frustration, then judgment and restoration.

God's knowledge covers more than the things that occur. But it never implies, in contrast to Greek ideas of God's perfection, something like a material or causal necessity for knowledge to become reality in all areas. Things and situations known by God do not become real merely because he knows them, for infinite knowledge includes knowledge of what is and what shall be, but also what could be, if something else were chosen (consequential knowledge); furthermore it includes knowledge of what could never be under any circumstances (counter-factual knowledge). There is therefore no guarantee or necessary link between everything that God knows in his infinite knowledge and the fewer events that actually occur in history.

We must not allow Greek ideas to creep into the Christian views. In Greek thought, a perfect being is complete. For Plato the divine was the ideal beyond all what he saw as the vagaries of time, action, and appearances. Aristotle's concept of God was a totally self-sufficient being, an uncaused cause, without any need. Were it not so, that being or god would be imperfect, waiting for events to occur and love to be expressed. Their gods never experienced anything new in the world of facts or emotions or reactions. Here perfect knowledge covers all reality.

Contrast this with the Bible, where perfect knowledge includes also imagination, fantasy, and even the lies of people and the devil. God knows them all, but outside the mind of God they will not all become real. Neither does God relate to them equally and without moral evaluation.

The God of the Bible is not a "Platonic Ideal" or like any lesser god of the Greeks. First there is true personality in God, who needs to communicate, love, and enjoy. It is not an imposed need, no late arrival in the development of God. God is a person who forever thinks, feels, and acts. Personality communicates, and that need is expressed and fulfilled forever among the three persons of the Godhead. Their love, pleasure, and imagination are eternally expressed, then brought into creation and expanded to include a covenant with all God decided to make when he said, "Let us make."

The Bible does not know the self-contemplating God of Islam, the Greek pantheon, or our modern ideal of radical individualism. Other deities are invariably loners, unfulfilled in any expression of true personality, sterile in power, and abstract from any real humanity.

Second, the God of the Bible is a God of covenants, of relationships established to expand into the created world the reality of an eternal relationship between each member of the Trinity. Having created human beings as well, God, who in his eternal being is gracious and loving, in a real sense needs his creation. For God does not back out of his commitments, does not write off his investment. He increases the value of holdings rather than walking off in self-interest: "God so loved the world that he gave his only son. . . ." One may not fully agree with ideas such as "the pathos of God" and the suggestion that God is the most tragic figure in the Bible. Yet the engagement of God to offer the Messiah as sacrifice for humanity's sin in order to remove both guilt and death shows God's faithfulness to the covenant of creation by means of the covenant of grace.

For God, perfection is not an all-encompassing totality that includes events already created by his creatures or those still to be created. Again, God's infinity describes the measure of his particular attributes: goodness, mercy, holiness, and love are some of them, but infinity as such is not an attribute. God's existence forever in the past and in the future as Trinity stands in antithesis to the separate members of the Trinity's possible non-existence. God created a world outside himself after the Triune God existed forever in perfection before creation and without it. They exist in a sequence of "before-and-after" forever in both directions, past and future. Yet not all events are co-temporanious to him. Reality is not an "Eternal Now" to him. There is always also a future to God's experiences.

God rejoices over good choices made on earth. He gives conditional promises to people and grieves or rejoices over the outcome (2 Samuel 7:11ff. and 2 Chronicles 7:17ff.). He makes the promise of the land, yet the journey took an extra forty years because of the unbelief by the exodus generation (Numbers 14:20–33). God knows what will happen to David if he remains in the city of Keilah and can tell him that. But God also knows that David will choose to flee when he hears what God tells him will happen (1 Samuel 23:7ff.). God can announce to Jonah that Nineveh will be destroyed because of its sin. When the inhabitants of that great city repent, which Jonah in a sense had feared they might do when they would hear of the impending judgment, the destruction never falls. One might also wonder what would have happened to Sodom if Abraham had pled for the five righteous people in the city and not stopped after interceding for ten.

These are situations in experience and history open to people and God, subject to real choices of all involved. They are not open or uncertain to God who knows the end from the beginning in all details. But they are really open, subject to the choices of personages involved. Only when prior knowledge by God is equated with necessary occurrence in some form of determinism is there a problem. But such is not the nature of God's knowledge, where the infinite knowing mind of God is not the same as the infinite Father in heaven exposed to a local particular event experienced by him and his creatures on earth.

A "Fateful" Regression

People in our own cultural past saw themselves caught in some fateful program. Today, people easily see themselves as part of a more mechanical or genetic program and have returned to this view. The intervening years of Jewish and Christian thought are all but forgotten, as if nothing has changed. In both cases real human freedom and significant actions by the creature are excluded. These views are held when we seek to recognize causation. It offers us both security and innocence. It is then convenient to blame God for all evil, but this is not in any way the Bible's view. Nor is it logical. Only when freedom to act is affirmed can moral judgments be made. If everything is part of a flow of causations, nothing could finally be different and all complaint is without justification.

Someone might object that the emphasis on human freedom in action is itself a consequence of a shift in cultural orientation, coming out of the Enlightenment, the focus on human rights and the liberation of humanity from authorities of state and church and, finally, from God. "Man is the measure of all things" follows Jean-Jacques Rousseau's affirmation of autonomous freedom.

But the notion that any real freedom to act comes from the teaching of the Bible first. The person who is able to so think of his freedom and insist on it, to protect it against the powers of past Fate and present State, is himself different from all parts of reality that are merely conditioned reflexes and effects of prior causes. In other words, the creature able to imagine, invent, and play God is himself free from the determinants of external causes. No other creature in the known universe is able to pursue as well as to pervert justice, to make art or make an ass of himself, to dream of his freedom and to dread a situation that is already determined in all its parts.

God is sovereign, and God has created a dependent sovereignty for us. Our freedom exists within a created order, but within it history does not follow a script already written. If Nineveh had not repented, it would have been destroyed. If Solomon had remained faithful, Christ would have been born through his descendents. If Judas had not betrayed Christ, we do not know who else would have done it. But of course, Judas had a problem with money all along (John 12:4ff.; 13:29). These are not theoretical "ifs" but the twists and turns of real history in which several actors make choices and in which God with sovereignty will bring about a real resolution without "doing violence to the will of the creature."

It is helpful to see that sovereignty as a concept deals with governance, not mechanisms. It relates to will and purpose, to ideas and power to implement these ideas. Sovereignty is moral and legislative. It is also implemented or executed within the reach of defined authority. God is God. Yet having made man a true and creative person with a derived sovereignty, God's sovereignty does not execute its power through every action of humankind. Not all history accords necessarily with the will of the sovereign God. For this reason God states the blessings and the curses at the end of Deuteronomy: the choice is largely yours!

This scripturally-proposed view of free human agency frees God's sovereignty from the constraint—imposed by Greek thinking through the centuries—to make God be the first and sole actor in charge of all events, to determine all things and therefore to make him ultimately responsible. Yet such a Greek view of divine sovereignty, fate or control is what is widely imposed on and associated with Christianity. When this happens so readily it will explain the reason why anyone who has seen the absurdity of life "under the sun" has good reasons not to respect or even fight such a god.

"Open" to Real Events

The teaching about the "Openness of God" is sensitive to this dilemma, addressing the reality of an open history, the need for prayer and wisdom to interfere against real evil in the forms of suffering and injustice. It rightly rejects sovereignty portrayed as the root of necessary occurrences and events. Yet attempting to get right up in the saddle of an old horse, it strained so much that it fell off the other side.

Openness theology has gone overboard. It recognizes rightly that in reality no human being can be a practical fatalist. We all complain, object, and cry out for a change. Some even pray as if it mattered. Not one of us is able to accept reality lying down. So we act as if we matter, as if prayer is effective in the life of God, as if God could do something about evil and pain. We write to correct error and fill in where ignorance left a gaping hole.

"Openness" admits the reality of historic sequences of events. They have not all "happened already" in the mind and eternal now of God. God and humanity come to experience and (in this sense) know things and events when they take place. This goes in the right direction toward a more biblical understanding of life in a fallen world. It confirms that Jesus did not accept situations as final but interfered against false reasoning, sickness, evil government, other sin, and even death. He did not play-act when he was troubled by people's problems or tired from his active ministry. Jesus on earth and the Father in heaven did face new and burdensome situations in real history.

There is an openness to history, a realization that life is not following tracks set in concrete. God is not finished with reality yet; we shouldn't be either. While rightly adjusting their view of life, history, and God to this realization and objecting to the determinism inherent in a narrow view of sovereignty, Openness Theology makes God ignorant of the twists and turns of future history, equally surprised and pained as we are and only capable of dealing with any eventuality by his might when it surfaces.

The problem with that view is that is reduces God to a bigger human—a cosmic older brother who suffers, grieves, and holds our hands in misery, because he has no prior knowledge of and little control over events. (Emmanuel, *God-with-us*, may indeed be our sibling, but to see God solely in this dimension is to have an impoverished vision.)

Determinism places everything under the total control of God by leaving out truly significant creaturely actions. Openness by contrast turns God into a pal, a companion, one who "feels our pain" but has no real control. Such a God would not know anything until something became historical. Genesis 22:12 is cited in this context to show that God does not know everything, including both the possible and the impossible. God, so it is proposed, did not *know* that Abraham loved and obeyed God to the degree that he was willing to kill Isaac until he raised the knife. But the text does not support this proposition which fails to make a distinction between knowledge as understanding and knowledge as historic experience. It is the latter, not the former, that had to wait until the knife was held over Isaac's body.

God promised many years before that through Isaac the blessing would come to Israel and the whole world. God knew, and so did Abraham, that the end of Isaac would not come on Mt. Moriah. Father and son would return to the waiting servants at the foot of the mountain (Genesis 22: 1–3). The knowledge spoken of in the text deals with the actuality of the sacrifice to God and Abraham in contrast to a known faith and commitment of Abraham to trust God to even raise Isaac from the dead. Abraham knew that this would not be the death of the lad. He knew that God does not require the human sacrifice so common in the surrounding cultures. He could assure the boy that God would provide himself a sacrifice. God in turn knows the heart of Man, knows the twists and turns of history, and can tell prophetically ahead of time what will take place under any possible condition. The knowledge God acquired on the mountain was the experience, not the insight, that Abraham actually trusted God in practice.

It is in this sense of actual experience that the word "know" is often used in relation to people and God. It does not stand against "ignorance" and is not limited to scientific insight in time. When Isaac knew Rebecca in his tent, the same word was used to tell us that they made love and became one. In Hebraic understanding, knowledge was always something in relation to concrete reality. Jewish people were not as interested in philosophical speculation as the Greeks were. "What does God say and do? When and where?" is much more important than what we, paying too much devotion to our Greek philosophical relatives, believe in our speculative mind.

Evil Gets Banished

We are caught then between those within Christianity who embrace with passion and their own vocabulary the old lure of a Greek idea of perfection, infinity, and knowledge and those who advocate the heroism of God and humanity in the face of an uncertain future. Who is in control? How do we fit in? Who is in charge here? Outside of Christianity and Judaism these questions are resolved with reference to one final determining power or glue which frees humanity from responsibility and blames "the other" in whatever guise is fashionable: all human experience is fully related to a god, nature, earth, or history. Any one of these made and willed it all. In that world everything has its place and purpose. You just stop thinking and accept it silently.

The alternative, what I call God's heroism, suggests more moral strength on God's part than creative power to act. In this case real history happens behind a curtain, allowing access for God and humanity alike only as directed by the script. The heroes, God and humanity, face monsters, but as each head is chopped off, seven more arise without any certainty of an end in sight.

The God of the Bible, however, is a fighting tiger rather than a gargoyle. There is a roar to his Word and a claw to his judgment, while fate, idols, and native spirits of the earth leave you with their cruel grin on a silent and ugly face. Heroes die eventually, but under the God of the Bible the battle is already won. Yahweh is innocent of the broken, unjust, and absurd world we inhabit. He has overcome the world.

CHAPTER EIGHT

THE INFINITE-PERSONAL GOD OF SCRIPTURE

A believing Muslim will tell you that there is but one God, that he is everywhere requiring obedience and that he will reward you with riches and pleasures in heaven for following the way set forth in the Holy Qur'an. All events on earth will take place according to his will. He is merciful and mighty and will judge the earth with power and reward the believer with riches and sweets.

Gotthold Ephraim Lessing and other Enlightenment philosophers have proposed that Islam is one of the three monotheistic religions of the world, which are so similar that with tolerance we should all accept the fatherhood of God and follow the commands. In the end Jews, Christians, and Muslims will discover that they all worship the same God. Like three brothers, they each have the full love of their father.

This idea is one of the foundations for teaching tolerance after years, if not centuries, of religious wars. There is much that appeals in this proposition. Tolerance of diverse viewpoints is an expression of respect and love, though the views still should be placed on the table of reality and measured for what they are worth in what they set out to explain.

It will quickly become evident that Judaism and Christianity also believe in one God who created a real world of things and people. But then the paths split and Islam goes its own way. For, while Allah is seen to be in control of everything with finality, Yahweh is not in the same way final. Yahweh created a world where additions, change, even laughter and lies are possible. There is life outside of God in the Bible, both in that the work of humanity changes what God had made after six days of creation and in the way that one can speak of a secular reality. "Secular" refers to what is taking place under heaven or without God. Of course, in one sense nothing takes place without some relation to the Creator. But in another sense, there is a reality of facts, choices, and events in which God is not directly involved because they are, first, the natural consequences of the original creation and, later, also the results of human choices.

Such a reality is not admitted in Islam. In some areas Islam readily seems to be a marriage between Jewish ideas and texts, on one side, and paganism, including the worship of the Moon crescent, on the other. From Jewish thought comes the idea of one God, a text to cite and obey, and certain stories of faith and obedience. From paganism comes the idea of all reality being part of one: earth, nature and heaven are all part of God. The moon's crescent, the symbol for Islam, is also the reminder of the moon cult in the Near East of old. In this intimate association of all reality, we find more paganism than biblical thought.

The God of the Bible is the creator of all good things, but they have an existence of their own, "according to their various kinds." They should be worked on and changed into greater variety. After the Fall they also need improvement and protection through human effort. This is part of the dominion mandate, which first encourages creativity and then, after the Fall, also demands moral resistance to evil and practical correction of a damaged world. We should not tolerate thorns and thistles, deserts and even death as normal, justified, or associated with God and his will for creation.

When we look out on reality with the clarifying insight from the Bible, we find the glasses we need to see reality in proper perspective. Scripture invites us to a realistic assessment of the sad and broken reality after the Fall. It does not encourage a faith that denies the problems, or dreams that are forever imaginary. It does not demand obedience to what is or to some unexplained divine authority. According to Scripture's unusual insistence, we should recognize that what is taking place among people and in nature is marked by the reality of death. It no longer corresponds to the perfection that God designed and made. No longer does God look at man and beast, nature and human nature and say, "Behold, it is very good."

We have already shown that the Bible does not present a God who planned it this way. His idea and its execution were perfection. The creature, starting somewhere on the eighth day and then continuing into history, created many new realities. Some of the good ones were naming the animals and discovering that Eve was not in any way one of them, but distinctly like himself. Their life continued in relationship to one another, in becoming one and enjoying God and creation for some time. But at a certain moment in history Adam and Eve also created a fallen world, a reality which has been with us ever since. But it was not forever in the past, and happily it shall not be this way forever in the future.

This does not mean that God is now absent as Deism taught. God has not made the world like clockwork, wound up and left to gradually wind down without his intervention or even presence. Neither is creation divine, though it is a divine creation. Nature does not contain God, but neither would nature exist without God's ideas and power to bring it about. God continues to add to what he made at first and what it became, through miracles and by his Spirit.

This is a very important factor Scripture insists on. Nature cannot be thought of as a world of naked facts, for they are someone's creation. Creation consists of ideas realized in material form. There was thought and action, word and matter: a real nature designed and realized. Heaven and earth do not only declare the glory of God, but they are his. At the same time, nature needs a continuous repair job post-fall, which all people are mandated to perform as they join God in his efforts to bring in justice, righteousness, and shalom. Human beings and ecology are creaturely, but humanity also receives moral instructions from God by means of language, texts, and concepts. Nature is impersonal, amoral, and suffering, but without emotions or moral judgment. Only people can care for the things of God and their neighbors.

I mentioned above that nature still functions lawfully and regularly according to the given pattern. By contrast, persons have a pattern that requires instruction to know what moral functions to select. Since creative freedom is part of what is inherent in a person, we require explanations on the right use of freedom. In the absence of an automatic program we require instructions about what is right, good, and just, for we function less by instinct than by discernment and making choices. This discernment has to be learned. We are not born with it or with instinctual responses to all situations.

The Bible instructs us that what is now normal is the result of God's creation having been affected by the fall of man (and Satan, but that is not our central concern here). It is abnormal in relation to what God had had in mind. Nature is no longer completely the expression of the divine will. God did not want people to suffer drought and hunger, catastrophes and death, inhuman governments and physical handicaps. These result from sin and its effects on all of creation.

The Freedom to Resist

The moral reaction, therefore, to reality bearing these masks of sin is to discern what *ought to be* beyond what merely *is*. Action is then encouraged to interfere significantly with "normality": first to resist a hostile status quo, then to withstand the tendency toward both fragmentation among people and finally death itself. Genesis 3 describes not only the Fall of the first human beings and its ugly consequences, but also the encouragement by God to resist, even to interfere with what has now become normal human reality and experience. All through the remainder of the Bible, God intervenes in word and power, with miracles and advice, with prophets and his own Son. God gives a different example to isolate the temptation and, for some, even the attraction to just give in, to bow to history, and to take direction for our actions from nature. By its sheer vastness, age, and uncomplaining silence, nature invites us to conform and submit.

Let us return to Job once more at this point. He must have felt like giving in at times; with friends like his, who can stand out like a sore thumb for long? Yet God praises Job, who insists that a normal reading of events would not be just or right in at least three ways. His friends suggests he accept his lot. He should hide his misgivings about it in humility and acknowledgment of guilt. The problems are obviously of his own making, and only his stubbornness keeps him from acknowledging the fact. Assuming a fair world as they do, Job must deserve such suffering.

But Job knows he is a righteous man who like Noah did not live like everybody else. So he insists correctly that God explain himself. His sufferings are not deserved. His experiences are absurd. Does God agree with the advice of the friends? Does he identify with the currents of Job's personal experiences and history? Is there no outside source of greater justice?

And the Book of Job shows us that the friends' assumption of a fair deal at all times is wrong. We do not live in a world of justice under the sun. Reality is larger than it appears to be. There is a second stage to history, where actions take place that have consequences on the stage of our life.

First, God does show himself, which is what Job asked for and what is so rare in our world. Adam and Eve were thrown out of the garden, and neither they nor their children and future generations are admitted any longer. So where is God? We live in a world of God's seeming absence. What does he have to say about this unfair human experience? Let him show himself. God is not afraid to give an explanation. God does show up to respond to Job in a way that honors him and sets him above his friends.

Then God explains that Job's friends have it all wrong to assume a fair world and a sound judgment. A fallen world is not fair. Their conclusion is too superficial, taking occurrences in Job's life as justified rather than looking at them from the perspective of life in a fallen world, where justice is rare under the sun. That is the biblical perspective from the start. Without it we follow the word of nature and history instead of the Word of God.

Finally, God turns to Job and reminds him that he was not there at the creation and therefore does not fully understand the complexity of the real world, both seen and unseen. There is a war going on, in which believers are falsely accused and where God endures the wiles of the devil for a while. Events on the hidden stage of real history take time. The accuser will be shown to be wrong but not until he has carried out his desire to prove God unfair, wrong, and unworthy.

Job is right to believe that this is an absurd world that does not in many particulars follow God's will or exhibit any true justice. God affirms this, denounces the foolish friends, and comforts Job greatly. The explanation transcends the events and places them into a larger context which includes the seen and the unseen as well as the past, present, and future.

You will recall that with the first two chapters of the Book of Job we become privy to that wider and more complex view, understanding more of it. There is a demonic accusation, which God takes seriously and deals with over time to defuse all the temptations of the devil and to prove him wrong. For the time being, God endures evil. I believe that one part of this is from God's patience, but there is also the element of real time involved in God's having to endure the choices of his creatures and their consequences before being able to weigh in against them.

What we learn from this and the panoply of Scripture is that God does not see reality and history to be the revelation of his will. God's will is found in his Word and what he originally created. The universe was good, for it came into being in form and content according to divine fiat. It is no longer this way, since the sin of Adam and Eve has affected all creation.

The Word of God gives us a platform from which to judge all reality. The world-that-is does not have to be accepted as necessarily final, good, or approved. Until death itself is swallowed up and Christ reigns on earth there will be no fair situation, no total justice for anyone, no area of experience to be uncritically accepted as coming from God. Nor should every possible experience offered in the market of the world or in the church be made, pursued, or embraced. Reality is too confused, often too dangerous. Like certain foods, it is often very appealing to the taste while poisonous to life.

The sovereignty of God is not affirmed when you believe that what happens in life is fulfilling what God has in mind. Only God's speaking explains what he desires and the kinds of things he does. God's sovereignty is honored when you live and work under his instruction, not under the dictate of events. Their power does not always express the power of God. That would be a very mechanical, material view of sovereignty-as-power. It would also turn God into one who approves of all things happening and sees them as good, fair, and just. Nowhere in Scripture do we find such wholesale identification between event and godly approval. Instead we find a God at work changing the course of history, leading people to repentance and a reorientation of their lives, pleading with Jerusalem to believe, encouraging the rich young ruler to follow Christ, healing the sick, comforting the poor, and feeding the hungry. Jesus' frequent laments about the disciples, those "of little faith," his anger at the tomb of Lazarus, his complaint about the unfaithfulness of Israel, and every other prophetic passage in the Bible addressing the beliefs and practices of his people would be senseless if sovereignty implied an immediate and unlimited power to accomplish God's will merely by willing it.

Such a view of sovereignty appeals to both mystics and mechanics. The former delight in the embrace of "otherness" and "wholeness" and see some hidden benefit to all experiences, including evil. They float on a rickety boat in a sea of great legal, scientific, social, and cultural uncertainty, hoping to arrive somehow refined through the whole experience, when in fact they possibly should have opposed the experience of illness, injustice, and oppression. The latter see in such a view of sovereignty a parallel to their world of computer buttons, binary instructions, and video games. Both fit into the pagan idea of the interrelated oneness of all reality. This view also does well in ages where sovereigns can kill their subjects with impunity, when there is no recourse to law or independent courts. It also works in a world where, with a push of the finger, you can annihilate the monster in the computer game without regret or accusation. But it is not the biblical view of God's sovereignty.

The point is that God is innocent of the tragedy that followed Adam and Eve's fall. The creature was free to love or withhold love, to obey or not obey. This is the only way that love and obedience can exist; if there are any conditions forcing the outcome, one can no longer speak of either. These terms require the element of originality, choice, and creativity—precisely the real things that are part of human beings bearing the *Imago Dei*. Anything less than this would be a controlled situation and would turn the human being into something less than what God made, a little lower than the angels, having dominion over all things created (Psalm 8:5–8).

Contemporary people, just as in previous generations, always try to find some external cause to be able to excuse their harmful actions. It always strikes me as curious that they will not similarly seek to explain away the good things they do. For these we want to receive credit ourselves. We only want to see the problems we create as inheritance from the past. We readily blame the stars in the heavens, genetic conditions, the weight of traditions, customs and habits, and finally also God; when it comes to causes for problems, we refer to something bigger behind us.

As I have suggested before, this is the nature of fatalism. It assumes a closed system in which one thing inevitably leads to another and in which nothing different could have happened anywhere along the way.

The Bible alone frees people from such a prison of all-determining forces and conditions and re-establishes true significance. In the Bible alone is the human being honored as a child of God and not a child of natural circumstances. Even when the king of Assyria is used as a razor on the head and feet of sinful Israel (Isaiah 7:20), the image does not imply mechanics, but war that will bring God's judgment on Israel, even as Assyria will later be judged for her cruelty and paganism. One can speak of real distinctions between right and wrong only in connection with genuine choices by free agents. Without them any differences are social, temporal, and cultural. Such variations are relative to the belief system of a small group of people at a certain time somewhere, held for reasons of their own caprice.

Why then do so many Christians find it attractive to read the God of the Bible into such a closed system? From whence comes the old habit of turning God into the original cause of everything? In the process of trying to maintain our own innocence, we turn people into less than what Scripture assumes about us in our qualities and our foolishness. Neither our goodness nor our absurdity are in any genuine sense real if God is in control the way Allah is said to be in control, or in the way such opposites as New Agers and materialists say the zodiac signs under which you were born finally control everything. The upshot is always that good and evil are only apparent opposites; in the end, everything is just in God's flow of things. Why not acknowledge instead an open field where responsibility for human choices lies with us?

Amazing contortions of the mind are proposed and required to include God in the chain of conditions that determine my life, including my salvation or condemnation. Many writers and preachers quote Jonathan Edwards to justify variable meanings of the word "will" in connection with God, so that God can be sovereign in the sense of being in control and at the same time hold me accountable. The Bible does not go through such hoops at all. They are unnecessary unless you wish to hold to mechanistically tight total sovereignty. And this is a vantage point foreign to Scripture.

Beautiful Notes of Dissent

When you join an orchestra that performs a composition from the world's religions and philosophies, it is required that you follow the same melody, beat, and tempo. There is a conductor to hold it all together. But why can't there be a solo as well, sometimes playing with and sometimes in opposition to the body of the orchestra? Why does the biblical view of God, humanity, and history have to accord with the fuller volume of the orchestra of world religions? If the great world religions play in some form of harmony, can Judaism and Christianity not stand out? Can they not sound a different tune, one in which God is an eternal person with a moral character, who thinks, feels, and acts; who laughs and grieves; who powerfully intervenes; and who will bring moral judgment on the lives of people and angels rather than weaving them into a seamless cloth of morally indifferent events in the passage of time?

It is quite natural that one wants to belong, to be accepted. Herein lies the attraction of religion and ideology. They provide a community of those tied to nature or history, gender or race, land and language. It is a lonely place for naked human beings, small latecomers in much of history. But to accept reality as it is and to play along with its melody already means a denial of human uniqueness and then of the uniqueness of the views found in Scripture. Jerusalem—not Athens, Rome, or California—is the place where God has put his name and revealed his Son. A community without a knowable God in heaven is a community of earth, blood relations, and time, all of which are ultimately impersonal and amoral.

Yet through the centuries, Christian apologists like Origen and Augustine led the Church at large into such accommodation. They repeatedly buckled under the pressure to conform with what such pagan views of earth and blood and ethnicity taught; rearranging the names and symbols, yet playing still the same old melody of earth and sky. They presented the God of the Bible as fitting exactly into the clothes made for pagan deities. They blended God with the Greek Ideal, with Hegel's History, with Voltaire's and Hitler's notions of Race. Consequently they lost both God and the divine image in humanity.

This is a bit like the overzealous shop assistant saying he has just what you need, only to pull out last year's shoes or jeans or say that this particular item is no longer made, merely because he wants to sell you something from the stock he has.

The pagan melody is the music of the spheres, the sound of nature, the remaining harmonious bits of creation's post-Fall clockwork. The solo voice from heaven was not often listened to. It has to be ordered separately and with some effort. Yet without it there is no real history as a process through choices, creativity, and imagination.

For that reason Islam does not know a purposeful process to life, work, and creativity. Muhammad is the climax of history; since then, faith is measured by constant and collective repetition. Islam is in its core an imposed instrument for the community of the right faith, not a path toward new vistas. For Islam time, life, and experiences stand still and obedience is the only area in which there can be change. It calls for the individual's adjustment to the status quo, not a moral and practical re-evaluation of both personal life and that status quo in light of existing problems.

The unique emphasis in the Bible is its historical emphasis, not only in the sense of relating events in time and space where they can be checked for their truthful occurrence, but also in the sense that history is not an inevitable program. History starts with God creating a purposeful world and continues with God's and humanity's continuing creativity, effort, reflection, and accomplishments. Your creative life will never end, there will be a judgment, your works will follow you (Revelation 14:13) and in all things your actions will have real results forever.

Sovereignty Revisited

Of course God is sovereign, but in a specific sense. He has created a real and lawful world, but he has not set down all future choices by those he made to be persons. There is no god behind God to dictate what will happen. But he has made creatures in the image of God, who are called "elohim," or "gods," because their real and significant choices should, but don't always, follow God's Word (Psalm 82:6; John 10:35). They can create good and evil situations—not against God's power, but against his character.

The sovereignty of God is established in the fact that only God is eternal, there is none other. No one else made him. Of course that is a major question, but it has an obvious and therefore quite simple answer. Since nothing existing in the world we know comes, from nothing, something must have always been there. For otherwise nothing would be there now. This "something" without a beginning, which was always there, is not a thing but a person. Only things can come from other things; but choice, consciousness, imagination, and the life of the mind could only arise from a person. A closed system of cause and effect can never bring forth any reality of freedom, originality, and significance.

God in the high order of Trinity can alone serve as the explanation for both impersonal things around us and real persons. Welcome to the world in which you are at home as a person. Persons are not misfits in a world created by a personal God. We have not evolved by mutation into realms of personality and choice from a world where there are no choices and no personality.

All things are present to God (his omnipresence); God knows all things, including "the end from the beginning" (his omniscience); and he is almighty, for he made the heavens and the earth (his omnipotence).

These terms require careful biblical understanding lest they be made light of and popularized beyond recognition, and lest God become again the "deus ex machina," sufficient for wishful thinking, but not true to Scripture. We have already suggested that omnipresence indicates that there is no place in heaven, earth, or hell where anyone can be out of God's presence. There is no hiding place anywhere. But it does not mean that God is in everything. God is not in my sandwich. There is space outside of God. This is a first definition, which is a "limit." (To define means to draw limits and distinctions of where one thing finishes and another begins). God is not infinite. He is the infinite-personal Creator. His characteristics know no end, but they are defined as love, wisdom, holiness, justice, truth, etc. God is inexhaustible in his love and justice, but he is never deceitful or unjust.

God's omniscience implies that he knows infinitely what is, what shall be, what was; God also knows what could have been, what could never have been and what could be, if a condition were kept or not. As mentioned before, God can tell Solomon that the Messiah will come from his descendents unless he turns away from God. He knows both and further possibilities, not just vague options, but any outcome depends on the real choice Solomon made. That alone could mean infinite knowledge. He can predict what will happen, including the result of each option the Roman soldiers had to abandon or to stay with Paul and the passengers during the shipwreck on the way to Rome (Acts 27:31). God does not only know these things theoretically, but sharply in his mind as real possibilities. And he knows what choices the creatures will make.

Yet that knowledge, because it is infinite, does not tie the hands of people to make one choice and not another. For God not only knows what will come to pass, but also what would come to pass if another choice is made. It is a Greek, not a biblical, idea that God's perfect knowledge requires that what is known must also happen. For God also knows the things that cannot ever happen in the creation he decided to create. Mere knowledge of things and events in God's mind do not inevitably lead to their occurrence and therefore to God experiencing them.

God's infinite knowledge of the past, present, and future is complete knowledge of real and variable options, choices, and conditional settings. Yet this knowledge does not make the future happen. The future is not fixed and frozen, for only when a future in time becomes the present is it the experience in real time and space. In the infinite knowledge of God, all future free decisions can be known by God in the same way that factually and logically impossible consequences of prior conditions can also be known by a God who, being big enough to have infinite knowledge, knows that there is for many known possibilities no way they could ever occur.

Why should it be impossible that "a future free decision . . . cannot be known ahead of time by God?"[1] The future is not an open question to God, neither is man locked into play-acting. There is a dynamic, but of several personages at once.

God's omnipotence in the Bible means that he is the one who alone made all things in the original creation. Other things also were made later by the creatures. This includes each of us as babies, made by one father and one mother each. We were known, but not individually made by God. Neither did two mothers or two fathers conceive us. Reality is specific, detailed, and known. Later creations by human beings—not God—also include windmills, domesticated animals, jet engines, computer chips, BLT sandwiches, and root beer. God's creatures made these.

God made earth, water, air, and planets in space as well as a man and a woman. He rules over sun, moon and stars, which were worshipped by Babylonians and Egyptians, by Incas and still today by the astrologically inclined. He set their templates and placed them in order. He made people and directs them not by instincts or templates, but by words of explanation, by language. He continuously acts into the course of history, from running after

---

1. Clark Pinnock's response to Bruce Reichenbach in *Predestination and Free Will* (Wheaton, IL: InterVarsity Press, 1986), 138 for repeated, yet unexplained assertions. With what reasoning, for instance, can Pinnock say that "future free decisions do not exist anywhere to be picked up on even by an omniscient being," when omniscience precisely states the opposite and all creation, free agents, and the lamb of God existed all along in the mind of God and then later became real in history?

Adam to answered prayer and miracles today. He is not the absent God. There is a Sabbath rest to come, but it is not yet. Here, too, there are limitations. God cannot do evil and get away with it as God. Were he to lie, or had Jesus not gone to the cross, God would no longer remain God. He is bound to keep his promises. Not that anyone is forcing him to do that, but by his own moral "limitations" he has tied himself down to not lying about them.

We must not immediately reject the notion of limitations to the God of the Bible. If you do anyway, you will run into at least three problems. First, you will not have a personal God. A person is always specific and distinct, with individual characteristics. All this would fall away if there were no distinction any more between God's love and hate, between justice and injustice.

Second, if God has no defining limitations in his character, all words about and from God would be meaningless. An infinite of any kind, even a non-distinguished God cannot be spoken about with defining terms. There is then no word of God, no communication of truth, at best only approximations. But an approximation without knowledge about what it is approximate to is meaningless. Liberal theology understood this clearly, but rather than rejecting it, its practitioners found satisfaction in the remaining and unresolved personal mystery beliefs.

Third, if God were not limited, he would be one with creation, for there is no room for anything outside of or beyond infinity. In that case you could not exist as a distinct person. All talk about good and evil as different from each other would be meaningless. You are left with silence as a philosophical answer you cannot live with in practice.

Such is not historic Christianity or the faith of Abraham. An infinite, non-specific God can grant no certainty or comfort, for to him (Would God then be an "it?") there are no distinctions of any kind. Abraham's faith and mine is based on words that communicate accurately. Abraham believed God on the basis of what he knew from both words and observations: promises spoken to him, including those about Isaac and descendents all the way to the Messiah; and experiences that confirmed those words in reality, such as Sarah's miraculous conception even though her womb was as good as dead from old age.

The Zen practice of silence is a more fitting response to a silent and non-differentiated infinite. It is not a silence of meaning, but a silent sigh, like the last bit of air escaping from a punctured tire. Without a specific, personal God, there is no way to go ahead. We cannot even name him, it, or anything "god," "being," or "power."

Silence! Real silence: no words, no complaints, no laughter or tears or holding of hands. No words on a page, no page in the real world, no real world.

Language always defines, draws boundaries, and thereby clarifies. That is why silence, the absence of language and concepts and even of "one thinking" (the "Cogito ergo sum" of Descartes) is the opposite to Christianity but not a part of it. Humanity in the image of God is very much thinking, creating, debating, and loving. It is a central part of that image of God.

In all three areas of omnipresence, omniscience, and omnipotence, we are dealing with specifics in relationship to the infinite-personal and personal-infinite God. The words describe qualifiers, not absolutes. We live before God. He knows and is able to be . . . God. With these defining specifics of God, we have not lost anything but gained the possibility of knowing for sure that God exists, who he is, and that he truly loves us in word and deed. "God demonstrates his own love for us in this: While we were still sinners, Christ died for us" (Romans 5:8). We have gained the possibility of understanding why things are so wrong in a fallen world, without God being in any way responsible for it. More than that, we have a God who is, in fact, furious about what sin has done to his beautiful creation. Evil, sin, and death are not a part of God's omnipotent acts.

Unless God is limited to being moral rather than simply powerful, there would not be any way to judge immorality, evil, and death. If God were in charge of all that happens, we could not call anything good or evil. Everything would then be godly, without differentiation from the demonic.

The God of the Bible is not sovereign in the sense of total mechanical control. Stalin controlled Russia through interference into every area of life and all levels of society. He controlled the Party by means of power, guns, and the fear of his people. This was possible in large part because of the oppressive historic experiences of Russians married to a platonic spirituality in both church and state. This prepared Russia for a secular version of what the church had taught as divine control before 1917, manifested then as historic necessity (Hegelianism) and "scientific" rationality (materialism).

Unfortunately, many efforts to bring Christianity back to Russia after 1991 have replaced the idea of the material and political control of Marxism with a flawed teaching of God's control without the liberating content of the Gospel. "Russians need to know that someone is in control" is not the Christian answer to their personal, social, and spiritual questions after the collapse of the central state and economic planning. What is new (for they have not heard something like it for generations) is an understanding of personal responsibility, courage, discipline, and initiative, and a God who establishes a covenant of favor to enable us to step out of fate, destiny, and the collective mentality.

Failing to explain this merely nurtures the historic dependence on central power, waiting on the sidelines to see what destiny, god, or the state will do next. Where we have, from our Christian past, the proverb, "The squeaky wheel gets the oil," the equivalent Russian proverb, from its resigned mentality and fear of being noticed is, "The tallest blade gets the sickle."

God's sovereignty then is in purpose, power, and ability to accomplish what he sets out to do. Yet each of these words has real definitions, i.e., limitations like any word. These limitations are not only real to us, but also to God, who is a person and not absolute faceless power.

God is sovereign in his purpose, but this purpose refers to specific realities. He purposed to have more than sticks and stones, impersonal functionaries according to template. God created human beings capable of imagination, choice, and freedom—all prerequisites for love and joy and consciousness. He wanted someone outside himself in his image, for sticks and stones do not love, listen, and respond. They just lie there and shine, blossom, or whatever their program tells them to do. Only people can love, discuss, search, and enjoy. Part of the purpose of God then is to have people with minds, souls, and intelligence as well as eternal material bodies. God's purpose was not primarily that we would obey him. His purpose was to surround himself with angels and human beings, so that he could love, enjoy, and talk with them and they with him.

Creation is a richer reality for the existence of personal creatures. Even sinful man is seemingly worth God's effort to gain the pleasure of having more than sticks and stones in creation. God's craftsmanship of humanity was not a failure and is still not a failure. He set out to display his image, male and female; it was and is a success. Just look around you. Do you not see human beings all over the place? Make a list of the good things people have done, invented, played for and learned, by whose efforts we live fuller and easier lives. The question of their motivation does not come in here. Just the facts, ma'am, nothing but the facts, please! Fact is, without human beings we would not be here either. And if only "believers" had value and deserved praise, each of us would have no place to start.

The creature is a disappointment only for what he did against his better knowledge with the abilities and form God gave him, not because he turned out to be something else, such as an animal. I can only become a sinner if I am first conceived and born a human being; that is my fundamental greatness, "a little lower than the angels" (Psalm 8:5), which I have now soiled *but not lost* through sin. The human being as a human being is therefore not a disappointment to God. God's judgment is not about being human, but about our being immoral, foolish, and unfaithful.

By referring to God's sovereignty in power I want to suggest that God is able to do what is in his character to do. He is the almighty because he originally created all things. He spoke, and it was. He sustains creation as well and made it in such a way that it will not contradict itself. God still creates additional realities by what we commonly call miracles. They are not freak events or events without an explanation. Just as God created something out of nothing so can he powerfully create additional things: lunch for five thousand hungry listeners, oil for the widow who fed Elijah, stronger cell walls in the body tissues for the sick. He can make blind people see, and we could make a whole list of things God has done to show his existence and power. He can even raise Lazarus from the dead, though that poor fellow had to die a second time later.

But from this it does not follow that God can do anything and everything at all times. Again, we would all say that God cannot lie, for the book of Hebrews tells us that it is impossible for God to lie and get away with it. He would be able to lie, but not retain his holy character at the same time. Jesus could physically refuse to go to the cross for us. In the movie *The Last Temptation of Christ* this possibility is explored through in a thorough and imaginative way. Could Jesus have decided not to go to the cross but instead to start a normal life, to marry someone like Mary Magdalene or Martha, have children, and then at a certain age die? Why not? It's a thought. It is even a good thought, for it is a way to show that Jesus really had a choice in the matter, which he himself expresses when he says that he dreads this coming hour, but then for that hour he has come into the world (John 12:27). And again a choice is real when Jesus asks the Father in Gethsemane whether there is not perhaps another way to redeem us than through becoming sin for us and facing its consequence: death and a separation from the Father in heaven in substitution for us.

So there are things that God can possibly do physically, but he would no longer remain the Holy God the Bible talks about. In addition there are also things God cannot do for the simple reason that God also has to exist with the consequences of his own prior choices and acts. For instance, God cannot make creation disappear, never to have existed. Once there, it cannot be erased. Having been there from Genesis 1:1 on, creation has eternal consequences that even God cannot do away with.

God also cannot make history go backward. *Back to the Future* is a film expressing a serious playfulness with history that requires more imagination than your unicorn. The idea of someone interacting with history past to create the marriage of the protagonist's parents is a wonderful mind game. But it is not history. I cannot intervene after my birth to arrange for my conception. History is linear; it does not go back and start over again in a different tract. God has made a covenant in a world of choices and consequences, including his own choice to create us in a particular way. Additional acts of God or humanity can change the course of history, but not deny its reality. There is no way of ever going back. The moment of the choice already made is forever and irretrievably past.

Much attention is given to the passages in the Bible that speak of God's repentance. But in each case the repentance is the result of a change in circumstances. It does not indicate that God changed his mind or that expanding knowledge led to a different choice by God. Instead we find that when people repent or Moses prays to intercede for them, the whole context has changed. The moral standing of the situation is now different. Significant acts change the whole mix of reality in all of life. God's moral relationship to a new situation is different from what it was before the significant acts of the creatures. God would not be moral or trustworthy if his relation to changed situations continued unaffected by the change. God is true to himself, faithful to his being and character. For that reason nothing significant leaves him in any way static, or unmoved, or stubborn. His "repentance" only expresses the changes embraced by God in light of his holy character to continue truthfully with the new situation.

God's repentance then is not an admission of wrong on his part, but the moral personal response to what human beings and angels do to change situations. When Israel sins, God wishes he had not called them. When Israel repents, God welcomes her with open arms. In each case it is the choice of the creature to follow or to refuse their Lord and Creator that affects the moral reality of God's relationship.

Talking about limitation in the Bible's understanding of God does not make God small, powerless, or subject to someone else's rules. It is rather in the nature and character of God, who has been himself—this specific God—forever. Another universe does not exist any more than another God exists anywhere. I am not saying this from personal preference; it is rather that the God of the Bible tells us this for the sake of our own confidence, trust, and hope. These would be meaningless if God or reality were different. In a world where anything could theoretically happen there would be no basis for hope, confidence, and trust, for nothing could be expected with any assurance.

Of course, there would be no basis for science either. You would hide in a cave against all eventualities, only to be crushed sooner or later when the cave itself collapsed.

God's sovereignty is grounded in his alone being God: eternal, good, and wise. God's sovereignty is not brute power, does not describe a closed system of controls, and is not outside of recognizable moral definitions. One further limitation is spoken of in the Bible. Both extreme Calvinism and the reaction against it found in the Openness Theology neglect the element of real time in defining sovereignty scripturally. The former makes sovereignty too inclusive and abolishes real significance for persons, as if God's sovereignty had quasi-mechanical consequences. The latter excludes God's detailed knowledge from his sovereignty and reduces it to his own sovereign actions in many new and previously unknown situations when they occur. Both of them hold to an idea of sovereignty without doing full justice to either Scripture or reality. Time, in a narrowly scientific sense, is a physical quality of creation. But we also have to acknowledge that for God to be someone—an eternal being with personality and revealed characteristics as the Bible depicts—God must exist in something like time. To avoid confusion with physical time and to defuse the emotional reaction so common when we relate the Creator to creation, one may choose to speak of a "before and after" relationship.

We have talked about a "time" before creation that is different from what exists now after creation. There is no "eternal now" to God except where people have robed God in Greek epistemological clothing. The God of the Bible communicates, loves, discusses, and concludes his choices among each member of the Trinity with his statement, "Let us create." There must be sequence or there would be no love, communication, exchange of ideas, and selection of options considered. Such is the God of the Bible who had not already made what he then made by divine fiat.

Here also Greek ideas have unfortunately crept into the teaching of the church, sometimes nurtured from apologetic interests wishing to provide Greek thinkers the answer to their idea of God within their definitions. But you can't squeeze Yahweh into a Greek paradigm. Augustine, for instance, made valuable contributions to the insight of the church, but he was also a prisoner to the Greek texts and bowed to the demands of his historical period. This can be seen not only in his views on human sexuality, but in his view of the relationship between God's sovereignty, human reality, and the question that interests us here, of time. He says about God, "Neither does his attention pass from thought to thought, for his knowledge embraces everything in a single spiritual contuition" (*City of God*, XI, 21) as if God's thoughts were not sequential, but simultaneous.

Augustine fears that sequential thinking would reduce God to finite dimensions and make him divisible. While reductionism must be avoided, a way should be found to address the reality of God's true personhood: who knows all things and the end from the beginning, yet who experiences reality in sequence as it occurs also in time and space. God knows things intuitively and not inferentially in his mind. But the creator of a real historic and special universe "knows" reality, in the Jewish and biblical sense, as a series of experiences in the sequence of their occurrence. In this sense time is not only a dimension of creation, but also relates to experience, to life, to personality. Such time does not come in measurable units, is not mathematical. Experientially speaking, at times, time can "stand still" or then again "fly."

I want to call this "time" before and after something. It allows for the fact that to God not all events are coexistent. God took six days of whatever length to create a multifaceted world. In the fullness of time Christ was born of a woman, as God had promised a long time before. The sin of Adam led to an immediate result in the legal sphere and a delayed result on the physical sphere. The children who would continue the human race had yet to be born before Adam's body would return to the dust from which it had been taken.

In a parallel way, the effect of the death of Christ had an immediate component to restore a holy legal relationship of believers with God. The delayed effect of the power of the resurrection in our lives will take time; it is still outstanding. Interestingly, Luke reports that Moses and Elijah talked to Jesus on the Mount of Transfiguration about his coming departure, his death, and resurrection on which they had placed all their hope for redemption. It was future in time to their lives, and everything depended on Christ's fulfilling the promise of the Covenant in his time.

As the fall had immediate and gradual effects, we are not surprised to find immediate and gradual effects in the redemption through Christ. Time is real, significant, and impossible to "jump over." God takes his creation seriously. To do otherwise would be a form of lying about what kind of a world he has made. We could no longer say that we believed God to tell us the truth about all of life.

But more than this, we also find that "time" is a part of God's battle for our redemption. It takes time to accomplish it. God is not the super magician in the sky who with the wave of a wand could do anything at any time. That is not what God has revealed to us. To hold such a view is simply an embrace of pure magic and pagan speculation. Let me tell you why I think this.

The Bible speaks of a battle in the heavens. The Lord is a warrior for us. Satan is seeking whom he may devour. An angel was unable to reach Daniel with prophecy from God before three weeks passed, and then only with the help of another angel, Michael (Daniel 10:10–14ff). In Job we see what happens in heaven in relation to and with effects on us. Job never saw this heavenly stage. We who read the first two chapters of Job see it there and also when Elisha asks for the servant's eyes to be opened to see that more fight with the Lord than with the adversary (2 Kings 6:17).

In other words, the time has not yet come for some things. God is the one who has designed this kind of reality. It is significant, though, that creatures also make use of time, add time, and disturb what happens in time. It took an extra forty years for the Israelites to enter the Promised Land because their parents, who doubted God's promise when they saw "giants" there, had to die first. Their unbelief wasted time for them, their children, and for God! God pleads with people through prophets, but they often refuse to listen. Jesus preached in Nazareth, but could not do a mighty work there, except healing a few, because of their unbelief.

God's dealing with people in the real world takes place in real history, where significant actions, choices, and consequences mark time and give it its contours. All reality takes place in "before and after" relationships. Time is not only a physical object. It is also a measure of how people distinguish between "now" and "outside of now," which can be past or future.

The important thing is to see that God not only created history, but that to God there has always been a sense and experience of sequence: "The Spirit had not been given, since Jesus had not yet been glorified" (John 7:39). Mary was not allowed to touch Jesus after the resurrection, because he had not yet ascended to the Father (John 20:17). But John also mentions that soon after Jesus had ascended Thomas was invited to touch Jesus (John 20:27). Jesus is the Lamb of God slain from before the foundation of the world, but not dead for our sins until he hung on the cross and was forsaken by the Father.

The other central affirmation in the Bible is that there is not one actor in history, not one controlling agent, not one significant choice maker, but several. God created the world for himself. But God also made significant creatures and gave them the mandate to subdue the earth, to have dominion, to give names, and to love. Fulfilling such mandates by choice rather than by template, instinct, or necessity would affect all of history. History in the Bible was never fixed in concrete or tied to tracks laid by God.

God's sovereignty is not affected by all the players, but they do shape history. Who will exist as someone's baby? When will the resurrection and judgment come? These are contingent on choices by a number of participants. The human "ifs" are of tremendous significance.

Think about how these "ifs" positively impact the emotional life of God. If God is in such control that everything already and for all times is what he intended, we have no truly grieving God, no man of sorrows, no sadness of Jesus when the rich young ruler walked away without believing. God has then designed what is now normal, and implicitly endorses what takes place at any time. In terms of ideas or philosophy, and how you see things, it is a modern variant of the same old pagan order, this time with Christian vocabulary. Life and death are then justified, as is my bad temper, your murderous tendencies, your near-sightedness, and your addictions. God then made homosexuals to be a mutation that leads to extinction, since they will produce no offspring. The commands to live otherwise, to bring one's behavior in line with God's Word, would be out of place, mere theater at best. There can be no room for praise, reward, and example if there is no real freedom to live. If all of life is locked into a script, there is no room for any real live people.

And there is no room for condemnation either: "I only do what I was meant to do. That is my destiny." And how interesting yours is!

But not according to the Bible! A command is always matched to a different future, near at hand or farther down the road, when the command is carried out and its effects become real by changing reality. Commands contain information backed up with a warning or power, so that any reality now is made to conform to what reality should be later. With God in complete control there would be no room for commands, only for comments. We would not sing, *Holy, Holy, Holy, Lord God Almighty*, but *Que sera, sera, whatever will be, shall be*.

On the other hand, where creatures can and do act, we significantly have much evidence of God's personality through his passions. We see God's sorrow, joy, and anger in response—in real-life interaction and relationship. When the Westminster Confession summarizes that God has no passions it has in mind something quite different from some modern readings of that text. The divines were living with human beings, kings, and other neighbors, who often acted arbitrarily, whimsically, and selfishly. It is of great comfort that God does not exhibit those passions. God is not even like the weather, unpredictable and inconsiderate. That is why the Confession, referring to the absence of passion, makes sure to affirm that God is not split in his emotions, does not have mood swings. Scripture reveals a God of mighty passions, real suffering and sound rejoicing over each person whose name is written in the Book of Life.

CHAPTER NINE

NOT ABANDONED

The infinite-personal God of the Bible is not an infinite power outside of history. He is not everything there is nor is he the only player on the stage. He is our heavenly Father, Almighty God, who tells us that our lives, choices, and prayers weigh in heavily to affect the course of events over which he sovereignly rules. He created the universe. The heavens and the earth are the Lord's.

Some of this ruling takes the form of having ordained all that comes to pass; nothing will happen as a freak event, without cause or in factual contradiction to what he has made. People will never be animals; apples will not by themselves grow on gooseberry bushes. The *tromp d'oeil* in an Escher drawing does not show reality, for water does not ever naturally flow against gravity. We all need to examine whether our eyes fool us. Corrective glasses put reality back where it belongs, and only then are we ready to cross the busy street. We also need to examine whether our minds are prepared to acknowledge that we may be face to face with a miracle.

When someone has acted, interfered, and done something unprecedented, we have no other explanation than that it was created. Every miracle is created by someone at any time. Miracles are present among us human beings when we catch a vase before it hits the ground and breaks into a thousand pieces. You decided to act into the natural course of events (*Fragile object approaches hard ground, following the natural laws of gravity, density and tension*). Laws are not violated or suspended in miracles. The situation changes because someone has chosen to add something to it. When you repent and decide to care for someone after all, that event is miraculous. God worked miracles when Elisha made the ax head float, when the sun remained for a while in the same position relative to the earth in Joshua's time, and when God raised Jesus from the dead, a first fruit of our resurrection.

Both God and people work miracles through their free choices to create an event, change a situation, or work into a real time/space reality. These acts are miracles because in each case a person did something that was not in itself conditioned by what was already happening. A miracle is an original and purposeful act. It occurs among human beings who are mandated to create, and walk the extra mile and surprise people by not automatically hitting back when they are struck on the cheek. It happens when Elijah denounces Ahab's sin, when Jesus does not cower to Herod, "that fox" (Luke 13:32). Miracles are creations by persons, whose lives and choices are not totally controlled by the material, psychological, or genetic circumstances. Persons set their creations into the free space outside of earlier reality by choices that are in some element "irreducible and unexplained."

The only answer to the question, "Why did you do that?" is "because I wanted to." There was no mechanical cause, not on the level of physics or on the level of softer influences like psychology.

God in his sovereignty created a whole world out of truly nothing and rested on the seventh day. He continues to act, certainly ever since the Fall. The human being, made in God's image to be creative, also creates from what God has made and what humanity had added to it in the power of our derived sovereignty, which we express through our own imagination and moral concerns.

Jesus did miracles to prove his claim that God existed, that he is God, and that God has not agreed to have the reality of a fallen world identified as God's doing or that it should remain the same forever. He is the eternal Word, become flesh to confirm God's prophetic Word as true, real, and alive. The universe is wounded after the Fall, under "the dust of death," where people are like sheep without a shepherd and where access to the house of God, a house of prayer, is controlled by entrance fees and ridicule.

God often seems far away, unapproachable, and hidden. Evil, absurd, painful and senseless events dilute any affirmation of God's existence. Bertrand Russell speaks for many when he senses that the twentieth century showed the absence of God. While others have advocated such a view before, our generation and culture are the first to try to make do without God.

Let me suggest that this may be related to the high expectations about the consequences of material and cultural progress. The twentieth century was going to abolish war, disease, poverty, and ignorance. The enlightened state replaced not only church and king, but also God. Enlightenment was now said to be the driving force behind all history, evidenced in human progress. After such optimistic hopes, the twentieth century proceeded to be the most murderous century in history. The heightened expectations did not come true. There is little divinity and much inhumanity in human beings. The unrealized promises from a distorted Christianity could then be used to discredit God, reason, and revelation. The mistake, though, was envisioning God in control of human choices and events. The fall of Adam and consequently the innocence of God in this tragedy were neglected. When God is seen as tied to human events without moral distance, God must share in human monstrosities; they in turn prove the absence of anyone like the God of the Bible.

This feeling of God's abandonment is not surprising. Some of it comes from being outside the Garden of Eden. Part of this feeling of God's absence is due to our very limited time horizon. Then again we measure "presence" by what we see, feel, and experience, all quite sensual means of reaching knowledge. Christ came to change this by his life, actions, debates, power, and ability to pay for our sins and their consequences through his death and resurrection. His observed, factual, and authoritative presence to reliable witnesses frees us from the need for an immediate daily sensual experience. Now sensuality can be replaced by understanding what makes sense, by believing with our minds and hearts, by seeing with our mind's eye. But the nineteenth century and ours demand positive material verification.

A baby believes that mother and father have disappeared from the earth when they leave the room. A young child will know they are still present, because they can hear their footsteps and their voices in the other room. A still older child will know from memory and an ability to abstract knowledge that the parents will come back when they finished their work. We grow in well-grounded faith as we gain more maturity and are able to keep a larger reality in mind than what we can see with our eyes or experience at any one moment.

We believe in the power of God without having to see that power manifested in all the daily events of life. We believe selectively, not in fate or destiny. We see the hand and mind of God here and there, through a glass darkly, but we do not confuse it with the power of men and women to create a very mixed history of good and bad choices.

The Bible reveals no lightweight or insubstantial God. He is almighty. "Nothing is too hard for you," Jeremiah exclaims (Jeremiah 32:17). God confirms this in verse 27: "I am the LORD, the God of all mankind. Is anything too hard for me?" Job confesses in the end (Job 42:2) his knowledge that "no plans of [God] can be thwarted." When Sarah laughs about the promise of a son in her old age, God responds with, "Is anything too hard for the

LORD?" (Genesis 18:14) It is worth noting that "hard" here can also be translated as "wonderful."

But what is not too hard, impossible, or insurmountable is always specifically described. It is not a general statement without qualification. We have already seen that the Bible talks about God's character being infinite in depth, inexhaustible, and unalterable. Yet this does not mean that God contains all possible character alternatives. He is only good, and his goodness does not come to an end. He is love without ever exhausting it. But he is neither evil nor indifferent.

If I were to sketch a visual illustration of this concept I would suggest a large pipeline. The diameter defines the limits toward the outside. Without such limits nothing could be transported through the pipeline. In fact, you would not have a pipeline—you would have a mess! But in length the pipeline can span the globe. Applied to God the limits that define the "diameter" are God's characteristics. Because he is such a god of precise definitions he can endlessly love, fairly judge, have boundless compassion and infinite power to do good.

In the same way, the declarations that "nothing is too hard for God" and "what is impossible with men is possible with God" (Luke 18:27) must be related to what is spoken of, promised, and in line with the known characteristics of God. These wonderful affirmations, confessions, and acknowledgments do not refer to random possibilities or the immoral, unjust, freak and weird powers with which pagan deities, spirits, and gods are credited. Their believers state this kind of limitless power and interference about their gods more from a deep fear in light of an apparently random and inscrutable reality. Jews and Christians affirm God's power from the comfort of knowing the goodness, faithfulness, and love of the Creator toward his creation.

The angel's statement, "For nothing is impossible with God" (Luke 1:37) speaks both of the healing of Elizabeth's bareness and

Mary becoming the woman through whom the Messiah would receive a body. The "nothing" is not a statement of absolute possibilities, but of specific moral and physical power to get a defined and necessary job done. Jesus' claim that "What is impossible with men is possible with God" (Luke 18:27) addresses the difficulty for a rich man, whose heart is set on his riches, to enter the kingdom of God.

In paganism, deities are responsible for what happens and may well be guilty, for they are mere projections by people of their worst insights about humanity, foisted upon their gods. I agree with the German philosopher Feuerbach, who suggested that religions are projections of the human mind. Gods and spirits only exist because I put them there. Greek myths and Germanic stories are full of such assumed divine presences and powers behind all happenings in human life. River gods, weather gods, gods of war, and divine powers behind sexual drives are all marvelous inventions to justify anything and shift blame to someone else. Such gods are responsible for the way things happen and the way people behave. They also vindicate the rightfulness of everything that happens.

But the God of the Bible is innocent of what evil occurs. He is not merely a projection of the human mind. It is rather the other way around. For Feuerbach to be able to make such a projection he has to be different from everything else, a human being with imagination rather than an animal with mere instincts. That difference in man can only be explained if the God of the Bible existed before there ever was a Feuerbach.

God had us in mind first and then created us in his image. We are different, capable of imagining gods that have no existence other than in our minds, because we have been made differently, capable of understanding the truth and of distorting it for our own reasons. We are people able to understand God's Word but also capable of tremendous cruelty, flawed imagination, misuse of power, and selfish insistence on occupying center stage. People are guilty of the mess we encounter on all sides. God is innocent of it, for his intervention is to heal, inform, and call to repentance, "for the kingdom of heaven is near" (Matthew 3:2 and parallels).

Jeremiah 32 shows us many of the areas in which it is established that nothing is too hard for the Lord. Not all of them are mentioned here, of course, but it is instructive to see how Jeremiah does not believe that even for God "everything" means "totally everything." Yet the power of God is so specific that Jeremiah counts on God and buys a field in light of the future time, when "houses, fields, and vineyards will again be bought in this land" (v. 15).

So what is God's "everything" in Jeremiah's understanding? God's specific power is displayed in creation (v. 17), in judgment (v. 18), with close attention to justice (v. 19), with miracles in Egypt (v. 20), fulfilling the promises made (v. 21), in punishment for sin (v. 23), including the Babylonian captivity (v. 24), in accurate prophecies (v. 28, 29), in separating what goes on in the city of Jerusalem with its sins from God's own holiness (vv. 31–34) and in God's efforts to fulfill his promise that once again "they will be my people and I will be their God" (v. 38). God "will give them singleness of heart and action, so that they will always fear me for their own good" (v. 39). God's might is evidenced in his ability to "[bring] all this great calamity on this people." But with the same power he "will bring upon them all the prosperity that I have promised them" as well (v. 42).

None of those things are too hard for God. Neither is it impossible to have Sarah conceive a child in her old age, since the Creator could even bring Sarah's womb back from the "dead" (Romans 4:18–19). It is not impossible for God to redeem us, glorify us, and bring in a new world of righteousness (Matthew 19:26), or for God to keep his promise that a woman would give body and birth to the Messiah (Genesis 3:15; Luke 1:37).

We must glory in the power and might of our God, Creator and Redeemer, but also carefully see that "nothing is impossible" always stands in a context. The double negation does not become an affirmation that all things are possible. The first reason for this limitation is that God has a moral character and deals with things righteously. Ephesians tells us that "God works all things according to the counsel of his will" (1:11) to sum up that God does everything he does in a certain way and with a determined purpose. He will accomplish what he set out to do. Paul is not suggesting that everything occurring is a work of God. The second reason for a limitation acknowledges the element of time or sequence, which weighs in once again at this juncture.

The Significance of Time

While all purposed and moral things are possible to God, they are not all possible at one any time chosen at will. In the framework of a real history, created by God, choices of God and of the creature must bear their consequences in real time or lose their reality, their true significance. Cause and consequence are not cotemporal. God knows already but does not yet have the pleasure of praise from a person not yet born. When an event or a choice becomes reality and bears its fruit, the time has come to experience it. We are again coming across the awareness that even for God there is a reality of "before and after," a time of waiting until prophecy comes true. Such a time was needed to see how Solomon would keep his part of the commitment in the conditional promise given by God that the Messiah would come from his line. You remember that because Solomon was unfaithful in the flow of his lifetime, the Messiah no longer came from Solomon's family, but from his brother Nathan's.

There is a second place where "time" is significant to God as well. Redemption did not occur immediately after the fall of Adam and Eve; all choices, good and bad, have reverberating historic consequences. Redemption promised, illustrated through the slain lambs during the history of sacrifices—initiated with God kill-ing to make garments of skin for Adam and ending with John the Baptist's "Behold the lamb of God"—is not the same as redemption accomplished. The latter had to wait for the "It is finished" of Christ on the cross where, forsaken by his father, he had become sin for us.

There is no way to wipe the slate clean. There is no cheap forgiveness or room to pretend nothing happened. "It is nothing," "don't mention it," and "that's all right" are phrases of social politeness, not of justice; at times they even promote injustice. Expressions such as these cover up continuing reality. In the real world, sin, damage, or wrong demand a sacrifice, a "doing without" on my part. I choose not to scold, not to demand compensation and now make do without, because I am willing to pay for a replacement or take on the occasioned pain myself. That will take place in subsequent time, during the rest of my life. Without the flow of real time involved in forgiving, generosity and sacrifice would be un-real and pointless.

The death of Christ could only take place after he had been born and explained why he was coming to die. This would make sense only after people had lived for some generations in the agony of a broken world. The resurrection could only take place after the death of Christ. God respects the flow of history and works into it powerfully, creatively, and in conflict with sin and its consequences.

Jesus did many miracles, yet in the span of more than three years we are told about rather few of them on balance. In some places Jesus could not do many because of the unbelief of the people (Mark 6:5). At other places he lamented the fact that people needed miracles to believe. In each case the miracle was a sign of something greater, namely that God keeps his promise about salvation by grace. No miracle ever resulted in all problems being solved. You remember that Lazarus even had to die a second time. Miracles served to support the message, the exposition of

God's Word, God's promises and their application. That is why Jesus did not feed the crowd on the second day as well. Miracles were not done to replace understanding and trust, real choices, and work. Miracles give evidence of the power of God, but they do not remove the normality of life in a still-fallen world. Our God is not merely a greater magician than pagan witch doctors.

This truth suggests a different conclusion to our reading of the Bible than what some churches promise today, on either the Calvinistic or Openness-of-God side of the spectrum. As often formulated today, Calvinism holds that God can do all things and concludes, when nothing happens after believing, prayer, that God did not want to do anything. It is surmised that such petitions are not in accord with God's will and that he had something else in mind; God's purposes are inscrutable and we are meant to continue as before. We are asked to believe this in light of the evidence that nothing happened. The flaw here is that they see God as the master magician and always trust their concept of sovereignty in the face of continuing evil, pain, and injustice. They rarely realize that their understanding of a real battle in the heavens has become theoretical and theatrical. If God could stop it at any time, why does he not do it? If he does not, willfully continuing our life in a broken world, is he not Bertrand Russell's powerful-but-evil God?

On the side of Openness of God theology, its advocates are sensitive to the reality of an unfinished situation, a real tug of war between sin and righteousness, between the accusations and purposes of Satan and God. They admit that God's has his plans, but that he cannot do all things, in their understanding because he does not know what will happen. He is at best big enough to deal with every eventuality when it arises, but he does not know what will arise when and where. Here we find a relative of Russell's good-but-weak God.

Both gods are imaginable when we start from events in life alone and then seek to make sense of them. Tethered to an earthbound perspective, we would easily line up with one or the other of these positions. Or we would conclude with Russell and a multitude of others that there is no God to speak of or to know. In this understanding the good, the divine, and the spiritual are to be found, if anywhere at all, in oneself in life as a pulsating force behind random acts of kindness.

The Insufficiency of "What Is"

The Bible's teaching, we need to remember again, lifts us off the wheel of fate and the determinism suggested in all religions outside of the Bible. Jesus does not identify God with whatever happens. We should remind ourselves always that we live by more than bread, for we find insight, wisdom, understanding, and orientation in God's Word. Life's circumstances alone do not teach us what is good and right. I cannot conclude from events in my life that I am on the right track, that what happens is the will of God or that I should be doing something else. Taken as a whole, reality is a constant reminder to question my life, but my experiences are not proof-positive indications of God's will for me. Only the Bible talks about the mind and acts of God.

Jonah's experience is a good illustration for this. He had information that told him to go to Nineveh. In the harbor he found a ship ready to leave, and he booked a passage. But it went in a different direction than where God asked him to go. He went through an "open door" when he located the boat. He should not have walked through it, for it took him away from where he was supposed to go. The word was the authority, not the travel option in the harbor. The way back was not through another open door, but through the open throat of a big fish that spat him on shore so that he could continue on to where he had been told to go in the first place.

Events in life do not necessarily constitute the will of God. It matters less how we feel or what we dream and imagine than what we know about details in life. I am not saying that events do not result from God's miracles and answered prayer. I am saying that any event must be evaluated in light of the Word of God and not in light of my wish to experience God answering prayer. The second command of the Decalogue warns against the use of God's name to justify our own vanity.

The Openness of God view rightly stresses the dynamic reality of God acting in history and history acting on God. It affirms that our choices matter, that God responds to prayer, that the outcome of many events is not set in stone or a matter of an everlasting script.

God in his sovereignty *will* do mighty acts, but be cannot undo the consequences of prior choices. He cannot change the fact that he created us as persons who have choices. He can act in addition to our choices and thus effect changes, but he cannot undo them. Perhaps the most powerful illustration is the fact that any baby you conceive will live forever. God cannot go back in history and retroactively prevent conception. Conception has happened in time, and time has now moved on: that person will live forever.

Another illustration would be that the time for one opportunity has now already passed. If you got up at seven o'clock this morning you cannot go back and decide it should be 6:45. It is too late, you have missed it; you will never have that choice again today. No time in history will ever be the same again. If it were not so, all our experiences would be an illusion. That is what Hinduism teaches: wishful thinking at best, insecurity and resignation at worst. The uniqueness of Judaism and Christianity has always been that it talks about reality, not fiction. To now attach to the word "sovereignty" all imaginary possibilities is to confuse reality and fantasy. It does God no honor when we believe our assumptions about sovereignty while we neglect what he has clearly stated and shown in Scripture.

In the flow of history we observe a give and take, choices and mighty acts by both God and personal creatures. The Bible gives images of warfare going on since Lucifer fell and became Satan. Our part in that warfare is to hunger after righteousness, seek justice, work in concert with what we are told in God's Word about life in the real world, and pray. We are to put the hand to the plow, to resist the effects of the fall of Adam, to live and repel death in any of its ugly manners. There is a prince of the power of the air to be resisted, defied, and bound. Until he is finished he is cunning (2 Corinthians 2:11; Ephesians 6:11–12), seeks to destroy the work of God (John 8:40; Matthew 13:37–39) and temps to evil such divers people as David (1 Chronicles 21:1), Jesus (Matthew 4:1,11), Judas (Luke 22:3), Peter (Luke 22:31), Ananias (Acts 5:3) and Paul (2 Corinthians 12:7). He is an adversary of Joshua (Zechariah 3:1–2). He robs us of the truth (Matt 13:19) and blinds us to the glory of God (Matt 13:17; John 8:54–55; 9:39–41).

Neither the Openness option nor the Sovereignty side includes in its reflection enough of the time's reality. The sovereignty view brings all events into the "eternal now" of God's final, inscrutable and supposedly holy counsel, so that all events are from eternity fixed and determined or at least controlled with all eventualities by God's power and choosing. The Openness view assumes that, because history is open, God must also be open to surprises, for God has a limited knowledge in light of significant undetermined actions of both people and Satan.

One theological system denies the reality of time to insist on sovereignty, the other acknowledges time, but offers no assurance of God's sovereignty. Each of these views is a step away from the biblical description of the sovereign God who is at war in time against sin and the effects of the Fall. Both views will use Scripture to support their claims, but the passages are always selected to prove a point. Reality, however, is not a collection of points.

Of course, we all quote Scripture when we talk about the teaching of the Bible. I do as well. But I also draw on the real experiences of every human being in the real and fallen world, for God's Word does not describe a theological system to impose on reality, like a presupposition that must be believed without the possibility of checking it out against the real world. Some on the absolute sovereignty side of the argument hold to "presupposition alone." They deny any real possibility of falsification on the grounds that man is too depraved to reason between fact and interpretation.

But certainly the Bible, in its language form and content, its cross references and quotes, its relevance to history, its address to people in the street and in church, assumes that there is enough skill and rationality present in the human being of whatever degree of depravity to examine and to argue with, to accept or reject what light there is to understand reality. The Bible is not abstract from reality, but it is God's word to fallen humanity. It is not written for spiritual people but authored by the Spirit of God to explain things for all of them.

Consequently, I cannot understand reality without God's Word. Christians usually agree with that. But I can also not understand God's Word without a deliberate honesty about reality. Problems arise easily when I inadvertently or by choice pursue one of these sources of knowledge and leave out the other. Both the Christian and the non-Christian have a problem here whenever they are not interested in truth but only in stating their "position." They have then both become ideologues.

From the Bible we see that while God knows the end from the beginning and all details in between, including those who will believe, he also knows all kinds of other things. I like to think, for instance, that God also knows whom my mother would have conceived the month preceding my conception. I would not be here.

We also see that while all the things God would ever do are possible for him, some of them are not possible yet, at this time, by tonight. That is of central importance in our understanding of God, humanity, and history. It is a reality set forth throughout Scripture and gives a much more scriptural and moral answer to the question of why bad things happen to good people, why believing people also die of cancer or why the wicked prosper while the faithful are persecuted quite often.

The recognition of real sequence and God's sense of "time" permits us to separate God's perfect will from the present situation. Bertrand Russell's conclusion that God is either absent, weak, or immoral is dismantled when we realize that with "time" admitted God can be present, strong, and moral without being part of the mess. The clean-up job is not done yet. The fullness of time for Christ's birth and death has come and passed. We are still waiting, working, and praying for the fullness of Christ's kingdom.

Romans 9:22 speaks of the fact that God "bore with great patience the objects of his wrath." We read of the seemingly endless patience of God with his unfaithful people: "Our Lord's patience means salvation" (2 Peter 3:15). In Revelation we are called to have much patient endurance (13:10; 14:12) in light of the continuing battle and before the coming of righteousness. It is part of the unfinished business the Bible talks about. We should not label "normal," "fine," and "in accord with the will of God" what has so many holes, so much pain and death at present.

Our common experience is of an unjust world. We all have both more than we deserve and less than would be fair. "Under the sun," between birth and death, there is no resolution. We believe that this is all the result of the fall of Adam and our later contribution to human sin. It is not God's work or desire. Our hope is in Christ's return at another fullness of time. Then God's judgment will come with real deliverance, for God will judge with power and justice. His judgment now is moral and not yet fully material. God is Lord and King, but his material kingdom will arrive when Christ reigns on earth. God has worked miracles, but these workings have never resulted in a righteous or resolved experience without continuing other problems later on.

As long as there is still death—and it seems that only Elijah and Enoch went to heaven without having to die first—we do not yet live in the world we look forward to, in which there will be righteousness. There is an element of "not yet" to God's work, for the results of sin are still material. The prince of the powers of this world will not be bound until "the elements" will be judged by fire (2 Peter 3:10) and only then will a purified world "be found." Then a new Jerusalem will come down to earth (Revelation 21:2).

This waiting in time, patiently enduring, is not like a holding pattern over the airport. It is a time of coming down into reality with moral choices and deliberate acts of courage and kindness. The Bible tells us that none of this is ineffective in history and before God. Your prayer, your actions, your skills, the time you take, the investments you make—these all matter. They literally weigh in materially and produce consequences. God, people, and angels act to follow the purposes of God.

But the lies of the "father of lies" also matter. Temptations followed into sin, choices made to deceive, idols set up and worshipped, people killed, and laws broken also give shape to history. Satan and people act to thwart those same goals we are called to uphold. This is the shape of the battle. It is not a program, where everything has its neat and purposed place. It does not follow the permissive will of God, whatever that was to Jonathan Edwards and his followers. Neither is history the fair punishment of sin; it is often not what everyone deserves in all its complexity. It is, however, the cumulative consequence of many actors and their numerous choices for and against God and his kingdom.

The battle is not between some eternal good and eternal evil, for in eternity past only God existed in the high order of Trinity.

Evil is not eternal, but a creation of the creature who wanted to be god. The choice for Adam and Eve was not between God and Satan, but between loving God and not loving God. They created a new situation by their free choice to discontinue the love, which had been there for some time. Adam created on earth a fallen world, parallel to the rebellion of the angel who became Satan according to Isaiah 14.

God knows it all and weeps, judges, and works with a mighty hand to offer salvation for the whole person, body, and soul. That will take time, as each situation is matched with God's resolution. Resistance must conquer each temptation, just as Christ was tempted in all things as we are, yet remained without sin (Hebrews 4:15). We put our trust in the risen Christ "to escape the coming wrath" (1 Thessalonians 1:9). By that we confess that God is sovereign, active with power and justice, in historic intervention and individual attention to his children. But we also confess that God is not responsible for all events now. Neither is he pleased with them.

"Providence" is a further concept drawn on to justify belief in the conformity of historic reality with the will of God. Yet reality runs according to the providence of God only in that things have an explanation. Providence does not suggest that the cause was fair, just, and beyond question. Providence indicates that God saw ahead, but not that God always approved of what he saw or even arranged it. It is a total misrepresentation of the God of the Bible to see in all events a revelatory dimension, as if God spoke through what happens. Instead God shows in his word through prophets and apostles how we should live, what we need to know, and when he disapproves of what people do. He shows how history proceeds and catches people unaware, exposing them to all kinds of situations, neighbors, and governments without any passion, pity, or purpose on their part.

Living in a fallen world involves life without a present wrap-up. There is no pretty purpose to it all. We have a bunch of contradictory, mixed-up, dissatisfactory, and painful experiences that people, now and in the past, have been and are always exposed to and either create or hinder. The package will not become pretty until Christ delivers it all up to the Father (1 Corinthians 15:28; Ephesians 1:10).

CHAPTER TEN

NO SEAMLESS GARMENT

Most people, including Christians, will see a purpose in all events in order to diminish by any means the experience of being strangers in a land in which they have no eternal citizenship. We want to belong and fit in. We desire to be imbedded in history, in a larger scheme of things and to see a purpose. In part that is what our minds suggest or even require. We see the effects of chosen acts and assume that all events happen for a reason. Whatever this reason may be—a reason from fate, destiny, the mechanics of a material world, God—each would avoid the conclusion of a senseless random occurrence.

Many Christians pursue such a purpose for events in their lives as the will of God and are insidiously willing rather to compromise their standards of holiness and reason than wait until the clouds lift and "shalom" to arrive. They prefer to assume that under God's sovereign guidance all things are already fine, deserved, a manifestation of the perfect will of God. Not so for the Jew who has a much more material and objective understanding of righteousness. Only when the Messiah will have abolished all swords, injustice, and death itself will the will of God be accomplished. The rejection of Christianity by many Jews is not only associated with fear of renewed forms of anti-Semitism. That is the somewhat superficial explanation. At the heart of much Jewish differentiation from

Christianity lies the rejection of the primacy of inner peace, the personal forgiveness of sin and a relationship with a Messiah who has not brought the peace and justice of God to the city and who is therefore much too private, intimate, and mystical. The failure to struggle in the outside world but instead to talk about forgiveness, grace, levels of personal improvement, faith and obedience makes it easy to reject Christianity. A true view of God's sovereignty should not give peace of mind but encourage a stand for justice, life, and reason in the continuing tragedy of human history. It should never lead to an acceptance by faith of events as the will of God.

Nature is not our home. "She" did not bring us forth; we have been created. We find with "her" no ear or heart to relate to; nature is not a caring "mother." Yet Christians want to discover God in daily events and are ready to see in them an expression of God's purposes. These purposes are seen as eternal not only because God exists, thinks, and works from eternity, but also in this way for many Christians they don't have to relate to reason, morals, or facts in space and time history. Yet when Christ came and actually broke the bonds of nature by healing a sick person, the herd of pigs rushed down the steep bank into the sea to drown. Our intellectual and spiritual home is with the God of heaven, not in the confines of a fallen world. There we would only be more complex neighbors to the pigs.

Feeling the Tragedy of Death

One reason we want to see a purpose even in the most monstrous events, like death, is to make them more acceptable. Look how death is made mellow in our days. We speak of passing and closure, no longer of death being an enemy. What is at all times a hideous interruption of all we strive to create in continuity is in this way somehow included in the bigger scheme of approvable things. The hard edges are rounded out and made smooth. Death is made a part of normal life, another stage, a different experience not to be missed in a mature life. Yet the Bible speaks of it as an enemy to be opposed through medicine and hygiene and eventually to be done away with through the resurrection (John 11:25 and 1 Corinthians 15:26). It does not disappear by denial of its absurdity. It does not become a friend by seeing a divine purpose in it or a door to heaven.

Death is not acceptable in itself, and no wonderful circumstantial consequence makes it any better. How many pastors do not twist the comfort of the resurrection into a pseudo-comfort, when they see God's purposes in death with reference to all that happened as a result of that death? In my experience, one pastor suggested that a handicapped child was given to the family by God to teach them patience; another said that a person died so that an unbeliever could hear the Gospel at the funeral.

These are ways to read purpose into unrelated situations. We do not go through all of life's ups and downs, absurdities, unfairness, and suffering to fulfill the purposes of God through all events. If that were so it would remove all needs to judge events, people, or situations. They are then all part of a major purpose. Yet the Bible clearly maintains a distance between what happens in history and God's purposes for history.

God's Work for Our Good

When Peter preaches (Acts 2:22) that Jesus "was handed over to you by God's set purpose and foreknowledge; and you, with the help of wicked men, put him to death" he does not set the two events in a rational, moral, or necessary sequence to each other. God did not hand over Jesus for them to crucify him. Instead God did what God set out to do according to his purposes. His purposes are explained right after the entrance of sin into the world in relation to redemption, the work of the Messiah as described in Genesis 3:15. A beautiful promise in Daniel 9:24 holds out a way "to finish transgression, . . . to bring in everlasting righteousness, to seal up vision and prophecy and to anoint the most holy."

When Joseph's brothers sell him to a passing caravan of Midianites, they take him for sale to Egypt. After years of favor at the court of Pharaoh, followed by prison and favor again, Joseph sees his brothers come for food during a long period of famine in Israel. Eventually Joseph reveals his identity and comforts them by saying, "It was not you who sent me here [to Egypt], but God" (Genesis 45:8). In 50:20 the same understanding is referred to again when Joseph says to his brother, "you intended to harm me, but God intended it for good to accomplish what is now being done, the saving of many lives." In no way does this justify the actions of the brothers.

They had good cause to be angry with their little brother and his proud assumptions. His fancy coat and intriguing dream about sheaths of grain bowing to him reveal a spoiled brat, a self-centered nuisance of a little brother. That he would later wear fancy clothes as Pharaoh's deputy and that his brothers would come to Egypt during a famine in Canaan to ask for grain repeats the earlier imagery and links the two events. It does not, however, justify Joseph's earlier haughtiness. By the time of the brothers' plea for help from Egypt's granaries, Joseph has learned to be a servant. He has become compassionate, loving, wise, and generous.

But how do we then relate various events, attitudes, and choices in their relation to each other? There is great complexity in any situation. Evil on the small level of Joseph's experiences of betrayal and acceptance is no different in kind from each person's experience of living with the results of Adam's sin and God's grace. To see these two parts linked in some overriding purpose is to remove the significance of each event or choice along the way.

Adam did not sin so that God could show us his love. Making a parallel to Joseph in Egypt, we cannot say that Adam meant it for ill, but God meant it for our good. Some fathers in the church taught this, though I suspect more from an interest to substantiate their attitude about suffering than from biblical studies or a desire to know God. Saint Chrysostom suggests in a famous sermon that but for the sin of Adam we would not know the love and grace of God. But this is again more an effort to justify a tragedy in hindsight. In this view the historic fall is absorbed by the future restoration. However, these are separate acts by opposing actors. Rat poison mixed with flour, shortening, and water will make a cake of some kind. Covered with icing and decorated with candles it would bring people together for the birthday feast. Yet we would not survive it. The apostle Paul rightly rejects the suggestion that we should sin more so that grace would abound.

Such a way to treating the problem is an attempt to seek emotional approval on the spur of the moment. It does not stand up to theological scrutiny or serious reflection. It results more from an attempt to approve, to leave no open ends, to find some grounds for the rightfulness of an event even if that is possible only through moral compromise and a denial of reality and reason.

Reason abandoned never brings the blessings of faith but always the tragic results of madness.

There is no room in the Bible for the teaching that the end justifies the means. No spiritual lesson learned makes the pain through which I learned it a good thing. In a good world you would have learned it without tears. A future improved or even perfected humanity does not justify the murderous transitions along the way. History never exhibits a smooth passage through time, no more than Stalin's murders were part of an inevitable advance of mankind. No amount of grace should undermine our understanding of real history; the glory in the end does not remove the horror of the past and present.

History is not a concept, an abstraction or a collection of parts in a common or unified flow through time. Several actors give it shape through their distinct contribution. Any attempt to see it only as a whole, finished and edible cake requires that we overlook the specific statements and acts of God against evil in support of good historic choices by the creature.

In the history of the Church such a view is related again to the thought that God is wholly outside of time. Yet God pays moral and passionate attention to details in time. No bigger view of God, making him exist in some form of an "eternal now" abolishes God's joy or grieving over real events, real choices, and real persons

Romans 8:28 says that "we know that in all things God works for the good of those who love him, who have been called according to his purpose." Evil is done, and we, "who have the first fruit of the Spirit, groan inwardly as we wait eagerly for adoption as sons, the redemption of our bodies. For in this hope we were saved" (vv. 23–24). The choices Joseph's brothers made were not working for Joseph's good. In fact they don't even address him as their brother but treat him as the son of their father's neglected wife Rachel. He must have groaned while sitting in the pit, being sold, then taken to Egypt and lured into bad situations. But God's hand was not shortened. Despite such evil God brought about something good. God remained the winner; the Lord will yet laugh and "have them in derision" (Psalm 2).

Separate actors are real persons who did different things to contribute to each moment in the chain of events that made up Joseph's life. Some, like his brothers and Potiphar's wife, did them for evil. God washed out the poison and interfered for good. For that reason we are told to rejoice *in* all situations, not *for* them without discernment. I am thankful for the true and good things I learn, but not always for the way I came to that knowledge. I am glad for God's presence and faithfulness, but not always for the circumstances in which I came to greater understanding.

The same interplay of human choices and God's actions, of clever and passionate commitments coupled with personal sensitivity to historic occasions, between God and an appealing personality, is found in the book of Esther. Mordecai is rightly alarmed and adds his voice to counter the immanent threat that through Haman's authority all the Jews should be destroyed, massacred, and exterminated. In a last effort he writes to Esther: "Do not think that because you are in the king's house you alone of all the Jews will escape. For if you remain silent at this time, relief and deliverance for the Jews will arise from another place, but you and your father's family will perish. And who knows but that you have come to royal position for such a time as this?" (4:13–14).

Wicked men do what they set out to do according to their purposes. Jesus announces his death in Jerusalem a number of times, much to the consternation of his disciples. But it would not then be perpetrated in Jerusalem because of God's purposes, but because sinners will falsely accuse, spit on, and even kill the Son of Man, who troubled their assumptions, power and rights. Their responsibility for their actions is not just an appearance of responsibility. They do not live in an illusion of choice while carrying out God's purposes like puppets. Reality is real. But so is the reality of God's many purposeful interventions.

One Play, Two Stage, Many Actors

The temptation for the Christian as much as the pagan is to seek a resolution already now to what is in fact a continuing tension. We would love to find a unified answer and a central cause for all events. We want to wrap up all of life and death, tie a ribbon around it, and present it as a gift from God. These images appeal to us for their orderliness. Questions would then disappear. We would no longer be troubled by unresolved situations that wait for the return of Christ. In some way everything would become bearable, because then we would know that we do not live in an open and unfinished universe.

But the Bible does not give that satisfaction. This would be oddly neat, and all things would have an obvious explanation. For example, Christians would have the will of God; naturalists, the power of the stars; Hegelians, the weight of history; American mystics, an unspoiled national destiny. Depending on what you believe is the final power, a seal of approval could be placed on what takes place. But it would also at once demolish any real difference between good and evil. There would be no space and time for further reasoning.

Instead we should relish the honesty of the Bible's view that there are several players. Both God and creatures act in history with real significance. God must and will do what is true to his purposes, his character and his power. He will interfere, create anew, redeem, persuade, woo, argue and finally judge. Jesus' statement that "No one can come to me unless the Father who sent me draws him" (John 6:44) describes the full work of the Father. "And this is the will of him who sent me, that I shall lose none of all that he has given me" (v. 39). There is no history in which God is absent. He has not died in the past, nor is he the absent master.

But the same chapter of John also gives two verses in which people are told about their obligations to act and to believe: "For my Father's will is that everyone who looks to the Son and believes in him shall have eternal life" (v. 40) and "Whoever eats my flesh and drinks my blood has eternal life" (v. 54). All four verses are tied together by the same repeated phrase "and I will raise him on the last day." They describe the same reality of God and humanity in relation to salvation and history.

There are always several players on the stage of history, and there is no common script between them, though they intersect at all times. Any understanding of history as a seamless cloth, a narrow road, or a printout of one author's text denies real significance, real battles, and real time. History can be sped up and slowed down, turned right and left, express more good or more evil being done on the whole. For history, like "mankind" in Marxist thought, is not a person and has no life of its own. It is always an abstraction until we admit that it is like the complex canvas or tapestry woven by both God and personal creatures. It has no mind of its own, no purpose, and even no direction. Thought, purposeful action and direction are initiated and undertaken only by persons.

Many will still say God must initiate all events in his sovereignty. We deserve condemnation, are unable to seek, have no interest to know and to believe. In the end it is all a matter of God's drawing people. Any of the human obligations can only be fulfilled by those awakened by God. There is, in this view, a priority to the work of God.

God places a priority on his grace, urgency, and desire concerning us. God clearly speaks of this through evidences of his existence and favor. But our dependency upon God does not mean that we are not inherently significant, capable of making responsible choices. God's grace does not make us alive as human beings but opens the door for being forgiven. The biblical perspective does not see people as junk until God lifts them out of the city dump for further use, receiving significance only at that time. It is not a scriptural view of man's "spiritual death" to see him as a defunct persona without an able soul, mind, and emotion until the divine encounter.

There is a priority for God to be God. He will accomplish what he has set out to do by his Word, by intervention, by judgment, and with patience. He alone can provide liberation. He alone can explain himself in words that can be understood. God the Son and God the Holy Spirit are sent by the Father to work in and among us in our fallen reality.

But God will not deny the created personage the choice to love or not to love. His sovereignty is not limited to imposing his power so that everything happens according to this will. It is rather an ability to do what is necessary to fulfill his purposes, often in spite of and at times in line with all we do on our level of derived sovereignty.

For our sin we deserve condemnation, but as God's image-bearers we are worth the highest price to God. The Bible speaks of a God who does not abandon his creation. He has invested himself in it and will not lose it. We saw previously how God gets back to work and on the eighth day, the day of Christ's resurrection, to proclaim victory and release of the captives. The grace of God is not that he has chosen some for salvation but that he genuinely has made salvation possible through Christ for all that believe (John 3:16).

This work is sometimes expressed as God drawing those who believe. John 6:44 for instance states that "no one can come to me unless the Father who sent me draws him." It is easy to assume that this is a picture of someone being pulled, perhaps even against considerable resistance. Some Christians have talked about kicking and screaming against the grace of God. Others imagine a bucket of water being drawn out of a well with much effort to overcome the pull of gravity. Many would see these as illustrations for the utter impossibility for humanity to know or even to desire to know the truth of God.

But that is not the only use of the word "to draw" in the Bible. It can also describe the drawing of a line in the sand to be followed, as in a treasure hunt. In this case it awakens a desire to find out what the treasure is. Jesus says, "But I, when I am lifted up from the earth, will draw all men to myself" (John 12:32). Jeremiah 31:3–4 speaks of God loving: "I have loved you with an everlasting love; I have drawn you with loving-kindness. I will build you up again and you will be rebuilt, O Virgin Israel." Hosea 11:4 speaks of God teaching Ephraim (Israel) to walk: "I drew them with cords of human kindness, with ties of love. I lifted the yoke from their neck and bent down to feed them."

The answer to why Jesus speaks in parables is given in Matthew 13:11: "The knowledge of the secrets of the kingdom of heaven has been given to you, but not to them." Yet that in turn is explained a few verses further on: "this people's heart has become calloused. They hardly hear with their ears and they have closed their eyes" (15).

The "drawing" then is in no way mechanical, since we are neither buckets in the well of life nor donkeys on a leash. It is not a force through chemistry or physics. God's efforts to convince us lie in persuasion, with evidence of power and reason, by God's gracious patience, through the work of God in history and on a conscience that is troubled by the internal contradictions in our beliefs (Romans 1:18–2:27). People are without excuse because they do not act on the basis of what they know. Instead they believe foolish things about God, humanity, and the world. Professing themselves to be wise, they have actually become fools.

In the Old Testament God draws people through evidence of his works (Psalm 19:2), including those through his prophets (Jeremiah 7:23; 2 Chronicles 36:15–17; Zechariah 7:7). In the New Testament God calls people through Christ, through preaching, and through his Spirit. He calls them "according to his purpose" (Romans 8:28), "for those God foreknew he also predestined to be conformed to the likeness of his Son" (v. 29) and "those he predestined, he also called" (v. 30). The first element relies on God's counsel to call people back to himself. He has foreordained this choice in relation to his creation and does not abandon either his counsel or his creation after Adam and Eve's fall. What is described is not an individualized calling, as one would call around to invite people to a lecture, movie, or birthday party.

It is not a selection process to eliminate some or to leave them on their own way. The Greek word *prothesis* means "intention" and describes the eternal relationship of God to his creation rather than an individual action. Ephesians uses the same word in relation to the work of God in and through Christ (3:11). In 2 Timothy 1:9 God is said to have called us to a holy life according to his purposes and grace.

This is certainly also Peter's understanding in his first epistle (1 Peter 1:1–16), when he talks about God's elect exiles of the dispersion in various Asian provinces of the Roman empire, "according to the foreknowledge of God the Father . . . for obedience to Jesus Christ. . . ." We should wonder what this might mean in light of the tension between external causation—as if fate, gods, genetics, or matter decided our situation—and the choices of a knowing God for our life in concert with our free agency as his children.

Jesus had already expressed the comfort for God's elect in the midst of the last days before the abomination of desolation in Matthew (See Matthew 24:15–31). Together with Peter, these passages might initially seem to indicate a selection on God's part of the elect from the mass of humanity. It describes a group of people who will not, in the midst of real persecution and hardship, suffer condemnation from God, though that is normal and common to the rest of humankind.

But the context in both passages gives us a wider picture than a holy—though to us seemingly arbitrary—selection. Both passages address believers in their present situation of waiting, while they see events by means of faith rather than sight. The way of salvation is not addressed in either passage. It is assumed that they are believers (1 Peter 1:3). Instead we learn of God's care for his children in the midst of their hardship, persecution, and a situation in which unbelief, rejection of God, and cynicism would be the normal reaction. Under normal circumstances people would give up, but through understanding and believing trust—through the very real energies of the Holy Spirit accessed through this trust—Christians will transcend their present experiences and believe in God to tell the truth and to be able to keep them in the midst of severe hardship.

Energized by God's Promises

Both Jesus and Peter address the believers as those who hold on to God's promises. In these promises they have something more substantial than God's apparent absence at present, the absurdity of evil in their surrounding, and the sense of hopelessness in the midst of growing evil.

In his letter, Peter reaches out to churches to overcome a situation of frustration that has remarkable contemporary resonance. Christians are strangers in many common experiences; they often do not have the weight of a majority in their culture. Peter refers to vast stretches of Asia Minor where they live but are not at home among their Greek and Roman neighbors. God has given them a living hope, a new birth (1 Peter 1:3–4) and an "inheritance that can never perish, spoil or fade." What they believe from God and about life cannot disappear into thin air as if it had no substance. It cannot rot while time passes every day. They wait in faith, and what they believe will not turn out to be useless in the end, ineffective like the grin of a disappearing cat in the branches of the tree; they do not live in Alice's wonderland. Nor are they left consulting the dead on behalf of the dead.

Instead believers in the Old and New Testaments have a hope of life, founded on the resurrection of Jesus in history. The content of our belief and the reality and evidence of God's power will carry us through to the revelation of salvation in fullness of time (v. 5). We rejoice in that, though we are at present without its manifest reality, since that will be in the future for us all. Your faith is pure and will result in future praise, glory and honor when Jesus is revealed (v. 7).

Anticipating this fulfillment in the future, rather than making decisions based on life's seeming emptiness on the one hand and unfounded religious obsession on the other, is nothing new for believers. Prophets, we are reminded by Peter, spoke for God when Israel around them repeatedly fell into unbelief and immorality. They waited like this at all times for something special in the future. They searched intently and with the greatest care, trying to find out the time and circumstances indicated to discern the timing of Christ's suffering (v. 11).

But now the time is coming closer, therefore they should prepare themselves for action (v. 13) in the hope of Christ's coming. "Live your lives as strangers here in reverent fear" (v. 17), for your faith and hope are in God (v. 21), who has chosen Christ, as a lamb without blemish and defect (v. 19) for our salvation.

In this perspective believers are elect, singled out, special, and precise. The context does not speak of the elect as an exclusive number, but as those who believe and are now called to carry out their faith in practice: in good works, in faithfulness to God, and in hope that in a future history real righteousness will happen when Christ returns.

They are elect, chosen, singled out in their stand and commitment to God, living now among strangers in strange parts, in minorities often, surrounded by all manner of foreign religions, shipwrecked faith, and immorality. Their special status is not so much one created especially for them by God, but one that singles them out as believers in a world of unbelievers, of being faithful in a mass of sensual people. They know God; their neighbors do not. They are part of God's people and as such strangers among Roman citizens by virtue of their different life, thought, and practice.

God's purposes are the heart of God's counsel, his foreknowing love leading God to pursue our glory. In God's own mind and counsel he decides on an action, informed by his comprehension of our need as his personal creation to whom he has given real freedom. Salvation begins with God and in eternity. God is committed to it all along the way to glorification. But the usual problems associated in our minds with questions such as who does what, when, and why or the relationship of human and divine will in it all are not addressed here. What Peter establishes is that neither is God's will whimsical or a matter of changing moods, nor is humanity caught in the workings of some eternal celestial fate.

Peter describes here that there is an underlying eternal counsel of God that is part of his character, which finds expression and application in the lives and history of believers. This divine counsel will bring them into eternal glory. By God's calling, his eternal work becomes a timely reality, giving evidence of his character. It's evidence in time is the fact that God will reign with righteousness in eternity.

The confidence of the believer stands against all of today's distressing reality, which at the moment seems to ridicule what God has promised. But instead of being left with a faith against evidence, we are reminded of the longer project and mighty power of our God. God's calling and foreordaining our glorification is surer than whatever problems loom large at present.

Christians are called, not constrained. This calling can be deserted (Galatians 1:6) and denied by making it a matter of obligation. God's calling persuades (Galatians 5:7–8) and makes us free (Galatians 5:13) to love. God calls us to lead a holy life (1 Thessalonians 4:7). Part of the work of the Son of Man is "to seek and to save what was lost" (Luke 19:5–10), but he is met with mixed responses. The rich young ruler walked away; others are urged not to receive the grace of God in vain (2 Corinthians 6:1).

God's calling is then neither a particular condition of life nor an imposed occupation. It is an invitation addressed to each particular person to look at the evidence, seek answers, repent and believe God to tell the truth about himself, the universe, and us as human beings. We are neither fully victims of our circumstances, nor selected objects of God's gracious picking.

Again, God remains innocent. He does not fail to call some, nor is human existence as such a failure to God or of God.

CHAPTER ELEVEN

EVIL: AGENCY AND INSTRUMENTALITY

And still, after an initial reading, certain passages in the Bible seem to suggest that whatever comes to pass in life is the work of God. For instance, in Isaiah 45:7 God tells us that

> I form the light and create darkness,
> I bring prosperity and create disaster:
> I the Lord do all these things.

A further double-whammy: Job's famous "The Lord gave and the Lord has taken away, may the name of the Lord be praised" (1:21) is followed in the next chapter with a question to his complaining wife: "What? Shall we accept good from God, and not trouble?" (2:10).

It is interesting, however, that we are then told that, "In all this Job did not sin by charging God with wrongdoing" (1:22) and in the same way, "In all this Job did not sin in what he said" (2:11), not as a result of some spiritual humility or from blind faith. Job never concludes that things are the way they are meant to be before God. He does not suggest or indicate that he has read events wrongly and now stands corrected. Neither does he suggest that God has a right to approve of whatever happens.

The whole text of the ensuing discussion between Job and his friends and finally between God and Job shows that Job's refusal to sin was seen in that he accepted that God would not do evil. Nor did Job conclude that if things happen they must be good, as if all things came finally from God. He did not switch back and forth between reality (evil) and illusion ("yet I will see it as good"). Instead, "Job did not sin" by maintaining a distance, against the advice of his friends, between what was happening to him and what would be God's work. He never accused God of doing evil; he never contradicted God's own moral character. But he did ask that God explain himself.

When we now look again at the Isaiah 45 passage we find that the evil, disaster, war, and calamity spoken of are brought on by God, but always in a specific context. This text and all the others do not speak of a god powerful enough to insist on his own right to do anything as a matter of physical force or sovereign right. Instead Cyrus is here told that God will do what he pleases. His pleasure is always in line with his character, with his covenant, and with his commitment to bring in righteousness. We are not presented with a whimsical God of doubtless power but doubtful moral coherence. He is precisely not the potter that does as he will on the spur of the moment as an expression of his whim.

God brings about peace and creates evil in response to what people have done in their lives, what nations have practiced in their moment of history. The acts of God are acts of moral judgment in pursuit of righteousness, justice, and fairness. The very next verse in Isaiah contains God's order to the heavens to

> Rain down righteousness; . . .
> Let the earth open wide,
> Let salvation spring up,
> Let righteousness grow with it (45:8).

God's judgment of good and evil will have results that are a blessing and a curse on people and nations in the long term because of what they have done in the first place. Judgment does not come from the whim of a mighty God beyond critique, but rather from a God faithful to his specific moral character. Isaiah set the stage before in chapter 43:1 where we read:

He who created you, O Jacob,
He who formed you, O Israel [says]
Fear not, for I have redeemed you;
I have called you by name,
You are mine.

To accomplish this God will judge the occupying nations who have violated Israel. In Isaiah 45 he announces that he will use Cyrus to free Israel from Babylonian captivity more than 250 years down the road. Jeremiah later announces that it will be at the end of the seventy years of exile in Babylon. On another occasion God answers Habakkuk's complaint about the same Babylonians, a "ruthless and impetuous people, who sweep across the whole earth to seize dwelling places not their own" (Habakkuk 1:6). The complaint is that a righteous and everlasting God has appointed them to execute judgment, even though his eyes are too pure to look on evil (1:12–13). The response is that the current judge of Israel, Babylon, will themselves be judged for their awful deeds. Babylon was but a razor of judgment on the head of Israel, but saw itself as divine, building its city with bloodshed and establishing a town by crime. Babylon, the corrupt judge, will be brought down, because the justice it imposed on Jerusalem led not to its own purification and faith, but rather to relishing its power even more. Babylon missed an opportunity to reform itself and to see the God of Israel as final judge.

Each step along the way human history will be judged rightly at some point, and all choices will find their resolution in time.

At any moment life may seem to be unfair and unresolved, but it is not random or eternally only a matter of unchallenged power. Righteousness will reign, and the righteous lives by his faith which gives confidence (Habakkuk 2:4) for the long run.

God's Power for Good

The apostle Paul quotes Habakkuk in his letter to the Romans (1:16) to set out that the righteous live by faith in the sense that they believe God not to be a liar. What God says about himself and the human condition as a result of the fall and the willful participation by each of us; what is spoken about the historic and legal way of forgiveness in Christ; God's commitment to give a new birth to his creation: all this is and will be true in the flow of history. "If God is for us, who can be against us? He who did not spare his own Son, but gave him up for us all–how will he not also, along with him, graciously give us all things? Who will bring any charge against those whom God has chosen? It is God who justifies" (8:31–33).

Immediately before Isaiah 43's affirmation to Israel that "you are mine," comes the description of Israel's tragic condition in 42:24 and 25:

> Who handed Jacob over to become loot,
> And Israel to the plunderers?
> Was it not the Lord,
> Against whom we have sinned?
> For they would not follow his ways,
> They did not obey his law.
> So he poured out on them his burning anger,
> The violence of war.
> It enveloped them in flames, yet they did not understand;
> It consumed them, but they did not take it to heart.

Disaster and prosperity, war and peace; when they come from God, they're moral judgments, not acts of brute power. His judgments are moral in the link between choice and consequence, cause and effect, significance and results, between crime and punishment.

All this is clearly laid out also in Lamentations, the book of sorrow over Israel's exile to Babylon and the destruction of Jerusalem. Lamentations 3:25–40 describes what is pious wisdom concerning human suffering. The passage starts out with a threefold repetition, like an affirmation, of the word "good": "The Lord is good," is the central affirmation; "it is good to wait quietly," for there is a reality of time; "it is good for a young man to bear a yoke," i.e., to learn, for suffering can have a multitude of causes, including my own past wrong.

> For men are not cast off by the Lord forever.
> Though he brings grief, he will show compassion, so
> great is his unfailing love.
> For he does not willingly bring affliction or grief to the
> children of men.
> To crush underfoot all prisoners in the land,
> to deny a man his rights before the Most High,
> to deprive a man of justice—would not the Lord see
> such things?
> Who can speak and have it happen if the Lord has not
> decreed it?
> Is it not from the mouth of the Most High that both
> calamities and good things come?
> Why should any living man complain when punished for
> his sins?
> Let us examine our ways and test them, and let us return
> to the Lord.

(Lamentations 3:31–40)

Returning again to Job, this is the reason why he could know that what was happening was not deserved or from God. He is introduced as "blameless and upright" (Job 1:1), which does not say that he was perfect or without sin. It does set the stage, however, to show that what happened to him was not related to his personal sin. He trusted God and only wanted an explanation to see how it all fit together. He was experiencing what we today would call multiple collateral damage. But this never shook his fundamental confidence that God is not the author of war, evil, or disaster per se. He craved an audience with God to present his case when hearing his friends distort the reality of his life. During that audience he also wanted God to present his explanations to correct the superficial view his friends were presenting.

That is exactly what happens in the end of the account. God shows himself, vindicates Job, and judges the friends as foolish in their simplistic view of God, life, and judgment. They, in fact, had been fatalists, failing to see the complexity of life in the fallen world, in which we not only inherit our own judgment, but are also exposed to the collateral consequences of someone else's bad choices and false accusations.

The same moral judgment comes on the King of Babylon in Isaiah 14, often thought to be description of the fall of the morning star, the son of dawn, who wanted to make himself like the Most High (Isaiah 14:12–21ff) and becomes Lucifer, Satan. Such lofty pride will result in being cast very low. He will be judged. He who wants to raise his throne above the stars of God will be

> Brought down to the grave,
> To the depth of the pit.
> Those who see you stare at you
> They ponder your fate:

Is this the man who shook the earth
And made kingdoms tremble? . . .
You are cast out of your tomb like a rejected branch
You are covered with the slain . . . like a corpse trampled
underfoot.

With that understanding one is better able to "accept with serenity the things that cannot be changed, to know what one should
try to strive for, and what one must settle for."[1]

It helps to put a moral grid over reality, and it answers the
basic questions life raises. With the biblical statements about life
we are not left with a play of power onto our weakness, where evil
pounds like the waves of an ocean on the unprotected shores of
each person's life. According to the Bible, evil already now meets
with God's resistance and the objections of each person with an
educated conscience. He who is Lord will encourage dikes to be
built in the present. When the Messiah comes he will calm the sea
as he did once before for the disciples in the boat.

Rejecting Nihilism, Embracing Life

Without the infinite reference point of a truly good and moral
God, one is not even able to make judgments, formulate complaints, and design programs to ameliorate the life people are born
into. Where there is no God, there is finally also no standard for
goodness. Yet if a tight link is maintained between a god and the
mixed and confusing reality of our daily lives, one must conclude
that either God has been a failure or I have failed in my understanding of reality.

The former of these two intellectual options allows at least for
moral protest, for in the human mind and in our daily experiences,
opposites cannot at the same time agree or be part of the same real-

---

1. Reinhold Niebuhr in *The Serenity Prayer.*

ity without doing the same kind of violence to language that reality is already doing to our lives. The law of non-contradiction requires this. The contradiction between life and death makes it abundantly real. A God who is together good and evil, at the same time weak and strong, who judges men and women caught in a determined situation as if they were responsible can only be rejected as nonsensical, irrelevant or nonexistent.

This is the existential choice open to us in the West, where we come from a history of belief in an absolute and moral God. This belief laid the foundation for our thinking and acting along moral categories. It also trained us in the sensitivity to moral and factual distinctions. It was a belief based on the Word, on truth, and discernment in reality, where answers to life's questions—both intellectual and scientific—were within the realm of accessible knowledge.

The second intellectual option is that embraced by Buddhism and other Asian religions in some form or other. Here all reality is part of a unified continuous flow, sharing a unity of Being. It can never be really expressed in words or evaluated along moral distinctives. Eastern religions propose a way into the world of dreams, denial, and submission of the mind. Reality as we know it is an illusion. All is finally One, and we are all a part of that one Being, a unified everything.

The goal then is to find a way to peace and quiet by way of detachment from the conflicts in reality. Faith becomes a way of seeing, by which reality and its power is denied. All reality then is ultimately an illusion.

Modern secularism or historic naturalism places everything on a moral slide, down or up. Its affinity to Buddhist unity is seen in the picture of the slide, or the river of time, or a moral void pregnant with opportunities. Every moment then has its own justification, whether Stalin's labor camps or Hitler's extermination program or the pursuit of personal gain without accountability to employee, shareholder, or the body of law.

Any real distinction between right and wrong, good and evil, Auschwitz and Jerusalem is only possible when not only historical, but also moral coordinates are used. They derive from the God of the Bible alone, then exhibit a practical concern for each man, woman, and child referenced in Scripture and found in each neighborhood around the globe.

Only Judaism and Christianity speak of a good God, powerful and sovereign, passionately involved and judge of the universe. The battle is real against sin, the moral guilt of wrong choices, and death, the material consequences of moral guilt. Real evil is present in real history and the victory will be fully won. Christ paid the price for moral guilt by his death in our place. Death will be conquered by the resurrection when the creator will make all things new. God has come to earth in Word, flesh, and spirit. And history will not continue sliding along forever. Not in your worst dreams, man.

A traditional hymn expresses all this so well and merits to be sung repeatedly with gusto:

> This is my Father's world, O let me ne'er forget
> That though the wrong seems oft so strong, God is the
> Ruler yet.
> This is my Father's world: The battle is not done;
> Jesus who died shall be satisfied, and Earth and Heav'n
> be one.

Maltbie D. Babock, 1901

CHAPTER TWELVE

MORE THAN ARROGANCE
AND RESIGNATION

Your view of the world, including your understanding of sovereignty and control, will always affect your way of dealing with life's realities. Your way of seeing life's building blocks is not limited to a private sphere, personal opinions, or your religious preference. What you believe about yourself, people, time, work, and more have very public results.

This is something we tend to forget. Since the Enlightenment we have made ourselves believe that what we've called "religion"—how a person relates to history and the real world, whether he believes in his fate or her destiny or their God— is a private matter with only personal consequences. The public life, we are told, follows other criteria such science and survival. Yet, in reality public life has been guided by visions, social ideals, and imaginative projects for an improved world, and it has used science to advance them. The religious ideologies of Marxist-Leninism, Fascism, secularism and the American Dream as ideas about humanity, history, and the world have exerted enormous and often very inhuman power over mind and body, over life and attitudes.

Ideas express how you see reality. They are like the glasses I mentioned early on, through which we look and see what we want or are made to see otherwise.

For most of our life we have known the unacceptable ideas of racial purification through eugenics advocated around the world—including America—before they were turned into a terrible philosophy of fascism that was defeated in World War II. Then we knew that the scientific materialism of Marx laid the foundation for Lenin and Stalin as well as the communist state with its horrible despising of human beings. They were atheists, we knew, but did we also understand that materialism leads to amorality? Or that without God there is also no image of God in man? In this view of life the only limiting categories for behavior are what can and cannot be done. The moral categories of what should and should not be done have no source in matter. The human being is all material, a means of production without soul, personality, or mind; a wheel in the large cosmic machinery. Power and weakness are the dynamics that decide the natural selection required for progress. And man becomes a beast to his neighbor.

Human beings do not fit into that vision. They have a mind of their own. They decide to work or be idle, to repeat slogans or write poetry, to steal as they are being stolen from, and to desire more than sex as a biological need. The materialist's vision could be partially maintained only by force and fear and by the police controlling what people thought, knew, and discussed.

But if all is ultimately matter, what are thoughts, knowledge, values, and wisdom made of? The reality of immaterial aspects of human life finally hollowed out the system when Gorbachev introduced the concept of honesty and people realized how much they had been lied to about life inside Russia and in the outside world. Where the people had not been honored, the economic production also failed.

Now we are directly exposed to Islamic views on public life, the economy, on politics and power, and we are largely puzzled. This is a religion: Monotheistic, communal, with times of high culture in its history. But we have not taken the time to look through its philosophical glasses, its view of life, its perspectives on control, death, work, and the place of women. We have failed to see that an untranslatable divine text cannot be debated and understood. It is repeated in the collective practice of recitation, affirmation, and veneration but never addresses the mind. Islam's high culture came more from exposure to Greek philosophy and Jewish culture, as well as more recently from Enlightenment influences, than from Islam itself.

Like Marxism and Christianity, Islam also claims to be true universally, i.e., eventually for everyone. But Marxism gave no room for the life of the mind and soul with its materialistic proposition. Islam proposes God, but imposes itself by force and fails to answer the questions arising from reality and human beings in it. Both Marxism and Islam are ultimately fatalistic in their outlook. In both philosophies the human being has no personal life, no encouragement of the individual mind. Both demand unquestioning submission to and acceptance of a historic or divine destiny.

We should have been aware of the power of ideas over the life of people all along. Europe's pagan tribes experienced such cultural transformation through the teaching of the Church that we no longer have indigenous tribes. Contemporary vandals are not descendents of that particular tribe that migrated from Denmark to Spain in the sixth century. They are just very naughty boys!

But we have experience with the failure of foreign aid, the frustration of relief and development work, the poor samples of democracy, and the tremendous suffering of people in cultures where their religious views have been left in place. African tribal religions, South American paganism, Buddhist attitudes in South Asia, the practice of Hindu rites, and nationalism revolve around ideas of how to see reality. They are glasses that do no justice to human beings, life and work, law and liberty. Pouring funds into a needy area does little to alleviate poverty when the human being is not encouraged to change his culture and to make it more focused on the individual person's mind, soul, and abilities.

The greatest hindrance to human development in Africa is the influence of its religions. Neither lack of natural resources, funds, nor people explain the continuing tragedy on vast stretches of that continent. When ideas take root in cultures they powerfully shape dominant attitudes and practices. They prescribe how time is used, what your attitude toward nature is, how you look at death, and, preceding all this, what you believe about the human being. Your view of the individual, of man and woman, of children and parents, is embraced as part of a larger religious landscape.

Of course, there is no mechanism at work here, but people's choices color their actions. It is impossible to make a scientific model of this, for people always present us with an element of surprise. We are pleased and disappointed with people when they are inconsistent. While there is no scientific necessity between crime scenes on TV and criminal behavior, nevertheless our mental priorities, the philosophical, cultural, or social glasses we wear leave us with real consequences in our outlook and behavior. What is thinkable has become doable.

Liberation from Oppressive Tradition

Of course, words like *choice*, *surprise*, *behavior*, and *priorities* each presume a measure of deliberate originality, real sovereignty and accountability on the part of each of us human beings. Yet I have proposed that a belief in total outside control, whether by a god or by history, by ancestors or by material nature, in most cases diminishes our sense of freedom, originality, and enterprise. When you see yourself tied to a giant wheel of history, kicked about by gods, or programmed by genetics and molecules, it is enormously more difficult to take initiative or to imagine that your actions may be wrong.

Daniel Boorstin[1] describes many cultures as marked by a habit of "again and again." He refers to the traditionalism and repetitions in daily life, in attitudes, and in ways of dealing with reality from generation to generation. These traditions insist on one right way of doing things—from birth to death, in work and celebrations, between men and women, in nature and culture. Obedience to an inherited program is of primary importance. By determining what comes next at a fixed time in the year or at a certain rite-of-passage age or in social events, considerable areas of life's insecurity are reduced. Traditions have settled how to approach various experiences of daily and communal life. There are formulas, patterns, and symbols that express a known content and meaning.

This habitat of tradition is appealing, for now life becomes manageable, especially where intellectual and spiritual tools are lacking to diminish the experience of so much uncertainty in life. Weather patterns and natural disasters, sickness, government power and even the length of one's life remain uncertain and are the cause of much fear.

The fear of the unknown and unmanageable can be reduced in the cultural contexts of habits, which become norms for a commonly accepted practice. Those norms then happen all the time. Everyone repeats them. Neighbors are born, marry, and die. Social and economic life participates in the cycle of things as each situation easily comes around again.

There is a sense of security in such patterns in the face of much remaining insecurity. Everything rises and falls each year with regularity. Like a summer breeze that moves thousands of ears of wheat in a wide field, people experience the push and shove of cultural practices. They make all events in life regular, repeated, and common. There are no worrying exceptions.

You get the picture. But the emphasis on community or collective thought and behavior makes it much more difficult to step out

1. Daniel Boorstin, *The Discoverers* (New York: Random House, 1983), 16, 122, 566.

of line as a person or to raise objections to inherited patterns. John Mbiti[2] writes about so many African cultures that know no future tense in their languages, largely because the future is but a repetition of the past. He adds at another place that each generation is watched by their ancestors to see whether they continue faithfully to repeat what has been passed on to them. There is ever only one right way of doing things. The very repetition gives security, as no past pattern is ever challenged or reviewed.

The focus then is on conformity, submission, and obedience. Reality is a program without an encouragement for novelty, imagination, or invention. Where the individual person is not given sovereignty over his situation, the situation itself will be sovereign. Many authors have noticed how much this attitude prevents people from developing as human beings. The mind is not encouraged to think anew, to explore alternatives, and take risks, through the teaching and repeated practices they receive from year to year. It takes a different view of oneself and reality to begin exploring alternatives and applying critical judgment or scientific curiosity to life's drama.

The pattern of "again and again" is embraced for many reasons: fear of being singled out as odd, laziness to pursue alternatives, or from a sense of hopelessness toward the possibility for change. V. S. Naipaul[3] is sensitive to such a cultural prison when he suggests that a person surrounded on all sides by mud and death has a much harder time to assume that now things will begin to change. It would take an enormous amount of self-confidence to stand up to one's neighbors, history, and fears, suggesting an alternative in the face of one's whole mental, spiritual and practical world. Their laughter may come first, mixed with hope for your

---

2. *African Religions and Philosophy* (Garden City, NY: Anchor books, 1970).

3. See his insightful discussion of these ideas in *An Area of Darkness* (New York: Vintage Books, 1981) and *India, A Wounded Civilization* (New York: Vintage Books, 2003).

failure, but the scary reality is that this could be followed by stones thrown or poison dropped in your tea from under the fingernails of neighbors or family.

It is encouraging that many people in such cultures will surprise us and step out of that kind of pattern anyway. Such a step always demonstrates the uniqueness of individuals, a certain unpredictability in the human being. It happens by choice more than by cultural pressure, when the cultural glasses break and reality shows its true face. Economics and suffering may play a large part in the decision. But change is often almost in spite of what has been held as "normal" in common experience, cultural attachment, and fate. Even the threat of "God's will" is drawn on to restrain a person from making a life for himself.

Yet it is remarkable that there is not a person anywhere who is able to live consistently with a deterministic view. We all praise and blame people as if they had a choice in the matter. We never just accept; instead we protest, weep, and hope like mad that our children will be in a better situation because of our efforts. We correct, teach, and encourage them as if such influence would enable them to make different choices. It is impossible for people to float for long like a dried leaf on the river of time.

In contrast to the attitude of resignation, submission, and an acceptance of a larger, closed, unalterable scheme or fate, the Bible constantly gives encouragement to individuals and families. Israel started as such a family of faith. The nation of Israel was repeatedly called to break out of a deadly rut, to review its past choices, and to create alternatives. The biblical idea of repentance not only relates to turning from social and religious error, but also from faulty views of humanity and God, neighbor and society, work and worship.

God's Unfinished Delight

Adam and Eve's original mandate to subdue the earth and to have dominion was to continue after the fall in pursuit of a more varied, creative, and righteous life. Both creation before the Fall (in what I have called an "unfinished creation" of six days) and after the Fall ("a world with a moral problem") were never to be embraced as final, repetitive, unquestioned, and without change. There is no exclusive "again and again" in the Bible as an approach to all life. We live in what is probably an expanding universe; in any case we certainly do not live in a closed one.

The emphasis of Scripture is on the need to discover wisdom, which is a very different idea than the value of obedience stressed in other religious and cultural contexts. Obedience is the conclusion, never the starting point of a responsible life.

When God spoke to Abraham in Genesis 12:1–3 and told him to "go forth from your native land and from your father's house," much more than a page turns in human history. Nothing will remain the same ever again. Until then God dealt with the children of Adam and Eve universally. Among them sin produced such evil that God destroyed by a flood all those who created lawlessness and wickedness among Noah's wide circle of neighbors. Noah was the one lonely moral man in a totally immoral society. His name, which translates as "he will provide relief" (Genesis 5:29), links him to the curse of the fall in Genesis 3:17 and speaks of his moral goodness and faithfulness in a sea of wicked behavior among the people surrounding him (6:5–7). This is given as the reason why Noah found favor with the Lord (6:8).

The flood did not eradicate sin. Sin continued to bring disaster, at first among Noah's children and then among a growing population. What God did through the flood, Noah's descendants then resisted through their own hubris or vainglory. They built the tower of Babel to make themselves a name. They placed their god's temple on top, where it would reach into heaven to honor the Babylonian moon god. They refused once again to submit to the God who made them. Consequently they lost the intellectual and spiritual focus for life rooted in the God of the Bible.

Their effort failed, for their god was not big enough. It destroyed their common meaning, their language, and their values. Their voices became a cacophony of opinions and opposing priorities. Man became an enemy to his fellow man. Each person designed his own religion, his own view of life and his own values. Abraham's father Terah became an idolater like most people (Joshua 24:2). In a delightful sentence the record makes clear that they assumed their building would reach heaven and by this accomplishment replace the need for God (Genesis 11:4). But then God comes down from heaven to look at this puny effort; at best the Tower of Babel just reached the clouds (v. 5).

But, as I suggested above, Abraham stands out of that crowd. He is called away from his father's house and from his nation. We must not understand that call as a strange zap in the night or a vision of light. More likely Abraham is talked to because he still believed in the God of heaven. That already sets him apart from his father's house and from his nation, from the Chaldeans (Acts 7:4). Their gods were of earth and fire, of seasons and floods, of fertility and death. But "these have no utterance, there are no words" (Psalm 19:3). Nature—including human nature, earth and sun, moon and stars—was thought to be divine, but from its silence there is no way to know that. People lived by sight and practice, repeating in their lives what was modeled for them in their natural surroundings. Paganism in its essential content is an attachment to soil, sex, and changing seasons.

Abraham, however, believed in the God of heaven, the creator and Lord over all things. The sun, moon, stars, earth, and its people are creatures, created things and beings. God's knowledge comes to the mind through understanding and wisdom; at first it is no sensual experience. Knowledge and wisdom are tools of the mind and heart, necessary to evaluate the experiences and patterns of what people do habitually in their culture. Knowledge comes from language, from words full of content, from revelation that explains our history from past to future.

Abraham's calling is not then a calling to salvation while he sat among his buddies repeating Babylonian or Chaldean rituals. Abraham was, like Noah, Abel, and many others before him, a single person who believed God to be someone, a person who exists forever and tells the truth. Language, content, and explanation would bridge the gap lacking in visibility. They would address the mind and train it. They spoke of a good and grieving God, who loves his creation and desires to be known and loved in turn.

No reference in the text suggests a form of selection or predestination when God talks to Abraham and tells him to leave his father's house. It was no freak event, no hidden mystery. Neither is Paul's conversion on the Damascus road a mysterious call from God. Such events, powerful and unannounced though they are, are not the expression of a selective holy counsel of God. These occurrences are no strange zapping, no weird appearance in a field, no contextless enigma. Paul's experience on the way to Damascus was wound around the core of his existence as he was seeking how he may serve the God whose Word he had studied as a Pharisee. He was given the answer to his quest, not an existentialist event. We are told that Jesus spoke to him in the Hebrew tongue, a familiar language to Paul in both the sense of understandable speech and coherent meaning.

God's calls are a continuing effort to make himself understood and to provide in history and through real people the Messiah's work and blessing to the human race. With Abraham God singles out one believing man's family and a multitude of his descendents. From now on it will be no longer the human race in general, but one man's faithfulness, personal courage, and obedience that will make history go in a different direction. To Paul, Jesus brings the fulfillment of his longing to know and serve God. He takes him from Damascus into Arabia for three years of private lessons about his Gospel before sending him all over the Roman Empire as apostle to the Gentiles.

I spoke for years with teachers in training seminars about Christianity in many parts of Russia during the first wave of interest in Christianity after the collapse of the Soviet Union in 1991. Often the question was asked why God chose the Jews as his people. I suggested that God had to choose someone, if a woman was going to bear the child who would rule and destroy the work of Satan. In Noah he found one person who remained faithful amongst an increasingly sinful crowd. In Abraham he found a believing and willing person. The promise to Adam and Eve at the time of the fall now gets increasingly more specific as to nation, tribe, and family, even location and time. The mother had to belong to some specific family first.

A Decent Neighborhood for Human Beings

God makes it plain that he chose the Jews, not because of their goodness, their power, or the number of their population (Deuteronomy 7:7ff; 4:37; 10:14–22; Jeremiah 31:3). He chose them because he loved them. His love was met by Noah's courage to be righteous and Abraham's counter-cultural willingness go be lifted out of the beliefs of his native Babylon. Abraham understood that creation was not divine. There is a God in heaven who speaks to our mind and informs us of his love and purposes by prophetic words and powerful acts in history.

God's call to Abraham contains more than a call to be the carrier of the Messianic promise. Abraham exhibited freedom to follow what he knew to be true. As a believer in God accepting his own responsibility, he stepped out of the confines of his father's family and his nation's cultural and religious patterns. He made a different history. He refused to repeat what was normal in his circle of neighbors. He did not look back to repeat "again and again" what was expected of him.

Abraham stepped out of the circle of repetition, nurtured by God's Word. Abraham chose to turn his back on any belief that earth or race, nature or stars, seasons or the movements of the seas give any indication of what is right, just or kind. And God "singled him out, that he may instruct his children and his posterity to keep the way of the Lord by doing what is just and right, in order that the Lord may bring about for Abraham what he has promised him."[4] Nothing as impersonal as the sun, moon, or sea could serve as creator and Lord over a personal being like Abraham or any one of us. Nothing impersonal could bring forth personality. Nothing silent could speak about purpose, morals, or meaning. Abraham turned his belief toward what each human being in God's image was meant to be. He would exhibit many flaws in his life; he would sin and give in through cowardice. But in his belief about humanity's place in history, Abraham was true to God's sure guidance.

The Western cultural context has continued this very different life attitude, distinct from what Asian religions, Islam, or the atheistic/materialist religion of Marxism have taught. Our culture is the child of Abraham's faith, cradled by a human family amongst whom thought, discernment, and restlessness express the sense of fundamental exile. People are not in all things glued to their immediate situation. They are not an integral part of a cosmic machinery. At best they give it momentum, change its direction, and use its purpose. The experience of exile comes from not belonging or fitting into anything other than what the Bible talks about as humanity in God's image, in need to know our true and living source.

We are not at home in the impersonal universe of even the most fascinating natural world. We think and speak, decide on purpose and direction for our activities. We invent and act, while nature at all times merely reacts to outside stimuli. We blame and praise others and ourselves, signifying our freedom between alternative ideas and establishing moral choices in many matters. We marvel and malign. We—male and female, old and young—are true persons.

---

4. Genesis 18:19 in *The Jewish Study Bible*, Tanakh translation (New York: Oxford University Press, 1999).

The Way Home

But now we are no longer in the immediate experience of God at all times, as Adam once was. On the horizontal level we are estranged from our neighbors, often from our work and from knowing enough about meaning, ethics, and human life as such. But God's Holy Spirit, who was poured out on all believers on the day of Pentecost, is God's gift, a seal of love and adoption to explain the difficulties and to enable us to heal the alienation.

Neither an infinite but impersonal, nor a finite but polytheistic universe can be home to the human being. We are God's creation, not children of nature. Scripture's declaration has created for people's hearts and minds a home base in God's human family, which he has made in his own image. We are also given in the Bible a recognizably secure and intelligent set of answers to the questions: What? Whence? Whither? Paul Gaugin wrote them in words on the back of his remarkable painting about the absurdity of life and the weight of a "cruel fate" he always attempted to vanquish.[5]

With such an open, accessible, and coherent historic text, God's people have a mandate to harness a wild and "natural" normalcy, which they accomplish to a considerable degree. Over time God will always try to turn our "nature" into "culture" through a critical process that includes review, critique, and competing alternatives. We have benefited immensely by what Cahill calls "the Gifts of the Jews."[6]

Through each believing person, goals are set for further accomplishments, refinements, and improvements. Rather than looking to be faithful to the past by repeating it, Abraham understood the need for faithfulness to an infinite-personal, personal-infinite God who was not finished with his creation after six days and who,

---

5. "Qui sommes-nous ? D'où venons-nous ? Où allons-nous ?" now hangs in the Boston Art Museum.

6. James Cahill, *The Gifts of the Jews* (New York: Doubleday, 1998).

when sin and death entered it, made a covenant that included a future righteousness. More than obedience is required in such an active, progressive, and self-critical approach to life. It demands discernment, effort, willingness for new beginnings, and, at all times, openness to critique from within and without.

This context has a number of philosophical relatives by cultural marriage, but the family name is individual humanity, male and female, made in the image of God. The mark of this family bond is love, trust, and enjoyment. As people we are reminded to love God with all our heart, mind, and soul and to love our neighbors as ourselves. Nature is not an accessible mother. She did not "bring forth" the human beings we are. Man became a living soul when God breathed in him the breath of life (Genesis 2:7).

Some would honor their Greek family background and emphasize the need to think, reflect, and take time out to discern. "Man, know thyself" is commonly associated with Olympus. The admiration for Greek culture, rationality, artistic ideals, and participatory self-rule themselves took central place throughout the last two centuries. It went along with the rejection of things Jewish and Christian. Rotundas on capitol buildings and columns on libraries, college lecture halls and even churches suggest this admiration for all things Greek. But culture, rationality, and the responsibility of people under God are in fact much older in the biblical proposition of our image-bearing and responsibility toward God. Abel, Noah, and Abraham precede Homer by centuries and exceed him in clarity.

Our Roman ancestors struggled for power and law to regulate human efforts and control the beasts within and without. Government by consultation between members of the noble families, the later republican efforts to compel citizens to live by law, and even the dictatorial powers at the height of Roman military strength and control over much of Europe and North Africa always served the purpose to gather people under law, and to protect society against barbarism and decay.

Later Germanic influences include the rise of heroism to change the course of history, to stand in the stream of events and cause such ripples that change would be brought about. Individual effort is not exclusively found among those who know humanity's exalted place under the dynamic personal God of the Bible. But common to this bundle of cultural life is the idea of review, change, and growing competence through competition in the arts, law, commerce, and even war. In addition, the Church's teaching introduced ideas of compassion, grace, and hospitality for the weak as well as education and law for a more civil society.[7]

History is made, not only suffered. Albert Camus said that none of us is guilty of history, because we did not start it; but all of us are guilty, because we all continue it. All of us, whether we tolerate it by lying low or whether we step in to give it a different direction, express a choice. We vote with significant consequences both by our silence and by our voices. There is no divine script, no first cause with limited and unalterable consequences. There is no destiny, not for the individual person, nation, race or gender. The belief in destiny's guidance is pagan. It gave rise to various enlightenment ideologies mentioned before, such as dialectic materialism in Russia, Fascism in Western Europe and Manifest Destiny in the U.S. The Bible does not teach such a closed system of inevitable history.

We are among many actors on the stage of history. People always have a need to express themselves, to affirm their individual selves. Artists sign their works and inventors apply for patents in their names. Children find separate identities from parents. We imagine a princess kissing a frog or invent a middle earth somewhere. We turn an old aluminum can into a vehicle, a goal marker, or a safe place for bugs we collect. We design machines, invent stories, and explore ways to improve our health, replace a

---

7. For a detailed and fascinating treatment of the idea of the West and its cultural roots see *From Plato To NATO* by Richard Gress (The Free Press, 1998).

missing limb, or find ways to clean up the environment. We try
out what we think to be better. Sometimes we fail, at other times
we improve a situation. We speak lines, write letters, lecture, and
find, just like the prophets of old, that people at times listen: some
laugh, others come back to hear more and some will even believe
(Acts 17:32–34).

The point is that Abraham was not a shepherd exposed to nature, which he then copied like so many others. He knew God to
be the Creator in heaven, for humanity was not just an extension
of earth. He thought with his mind, trembled in uncertainties, dug
wells in an arid land to draw water for his sheep; he betrayed his
wife in Egypt and laughed when he was promised a child in Sarah's
old age, even after he had made a bit of a mess of that promise
from God by fathering Ishmael with a maid. But he never took all
that to be his destiny. Obedience to destiny knows neither initiative nor repentance or praise. Its impersonal amorality prepares the
slippery slope to uncontrolled personal immorality.

The biblical influence in the human race is intellectual and
moral. It is rooted in understanding gained from a drive to see how
reality stacks up. Across the distance of God, subsequent to the fall
and our eviction from Eden, this influence comes through powerful acts of God and through clarifying language. The text is like
letters from a distant friend, addressing the mind, creating images
of an alternative life yet to be created by invention, by the deliberate pursuit of what is also possible and moral, to further human life
constantly threatened by barbarism now and by death eventually.

Culturally Judaism and Christianity have produced a mentality of change, personal effort, and responsibility coupled with critique, repentance, and dissatisfaction. We are aliens in this land because our home is not on earth in its present form. Compassion for
the weak, assistance to the needy, the rule of law to restrain harmful power, and many other initiatives create a world that produces
enough food for the hungry and gives hope to the exploited.

The God of the Bible is innocent of the evil in our world. Christians are not drugged into faith by an opiate of religion that makes them see no evil and resign themselves to their present experience. Jews and Christians find in Scripture a freedom from any form of determinism. They are called to love God and obey him, not through uncritical resigned submission but from wisdom and enjoyment.

The Westminster Shorter Catechism expresses this so well in its first question and answer: "What is the chief end of Man? Man's chief end is to glorify God and to enjoy him forever."

In God's words and acts they see encouragement to distance themselves by means of wisdom and integrity from whatever happens or comes to pass around them. This helps us raise questions against the tendency to see life as determined. We are helped to reject as final and without critique any setting that has as its justification naturalistic or divine, cultural or religious authorities and assumptions.

If God is tied to any status quo, he must be accused of being immoral. Any moral person would be constrained to oppose the dictate of such a god, history, or destiny. Enlightened Muslims flee their societies in order to be human in cultures born from a Christian and Jewish view of life. Dissidents opposed the dictates of the state and Marxist pseudo-science through their writings, sometimes even by feigning insanity. In response to the controlling God of what is falsely seen as Christianity, many in our societies have abandoned Christianity for similar moral and intellectual reasons. They would rather be fully human atheists than a certain kind of Calvinist tied by election to an unquestionable God in charge of a questionable world.

Neither Arrogance Nor Denial

In the past we replaced fearsome and questionable ghosts, spirits, and superstition with reasonable faith in a moral God revealed through Scripture and grace in Jesus Christ. Recent generations have abandoned the "God is in control" of Calvinism, because of God's implied complicity in or absence from the horrors of the twentieth century. They also rightly reject the immorality of some Christians who claim to have Jesus in their heart. But they have fallen into two new forms of determinism.

The first kind of determinism leads to a fatalistic acceptance of whatever is. Here people submit to a larger whole, a unity of being. That determining unity may be gender, race, color, or social context. These give a new constraint to people who thought they had been newly emancipated from God. Postmodernism opens with the discovery of relative moral and intellectual freedom. Yet it is in fact a deception by which we often become set apart into a variety of groups of people "like us," not free individuals. The group then demands obedience either by nature or expected conformity. The non-conformist is expected to conform in his nonconformism. Gender, color, and social background tell him or her what behavior conforms to his gender, color, and social destiny. We have seen this before in the propositions of fascism, nationalism, and forms of biological control.

A second new form of determinism seems closer to Christianity. It does not lead to fatalistic resignation, but to its opposite. Arrogance becomes the problem when the autonomous person with his personal or national priorities readily uses "God" to justify his own vanity. Here the unity lies in the belief that what I think and do or what happens to me is the will of God. Such a person can claim to fulfill God's will without having to consider that she may be wrong or may be following an imagined will of God, or in the end even an imagined god. On a personal level such an appeal to God's will protects me against all criticism. The arrogant (from Latin, meaning *non-questioning*) assumption is that I am right, because my God is right and God told me so.

This novel way of using a personal relationship with God in a culture that is in love with constitutionally guaranteed personal rights tempts any individual to absolutize his convictions and to see his life as his calling or destiny. All actions, all conditions, my place in life, my sexuality, my shopping and eating habits are all colored by the belief that I have a right from God to be who I am and do what I can pay for or get on credit. Israel thought like this at times, even when she abandoned her treaty relations to God (what the Bible calls a covenant), her obligations and privileges, her rights, duties, and accountability. In a personal, i.e., private, relationship to God, it is too easy to assume that all my life is a manifestation of the will of God and all my experiences originate from God's will. That is a closed system of divine demagogy.

On a national level such belief is found in a view of the divine rights of kings, racial superiority, or in "manifest destiny." Has God favored the Swiss by giving them mountains? Had he called Germany to purify the Aryan race? Have Russians suffered to protect Europe against the Yellow Hordes? Has America been chosen by God to bring freedom and market economics to the rest of the world? An appeal to a high calling or a sweeping "final solution" easily covers a multitude of personal and national sins by supporting what is believed and done, for better and for worse.

The belief that life is already a manifestation of God's will prevents any moral and intellectual critique from the outside. It turns events into revelation that is no longer under the control of the Word of God. It feeds on bread, not on the Word. Feeling right about something is not the same as *being* right in relation to a bigger reality now and the judgment of God later. In a fallen world, nothing—be it particular governments, marriage roles, job successes or failures, pains of illness or ways of dying, intelligence or stupidity—is necessarily from God. Different outside criteria need to be brought in to evaluate each and every experience. Nothing is determined in such a way that God should be drawn into it through praise or blame, unless it is directly the result of God's actions.

Even an assumed answer to prayer may be just as easily from my imagination as from God. We should at all times tread much more carefully and humbly, asking for wisdom to understand the times and situations in the complex reality of life in a fallen world that waits for righteousness in a new Jerusalem.

Until then, men and women will justify all kinds of evil with reference to God's will. Belief in reality as fulfillment of God's will leads as often into resignation and fatalism as it does to cruelty and fanaticism. Belief in God's control frees me from responsibility and justifies whatever I do, whether it is nothing or anything.

The command against the use of God's name for vanity speaks against any flippant readiness to claim divine authority in order to no longer question what is going on. Such frivolous appropriation is too easy a way to claim authority in a fallen world where God is not walking in the garden with us anymore. We are left with his Word and Spirit only. Not all events are from God or always good for us. Success, happiness, and peace may be just as easily manifestations of greed, shallow indifference, and individualism. To embrace them with unexamined faith is always irresponsibly foolish.

Believing something does not make it true or right. God is not necessarily on my side. Arrogance is as often a sign of ignorance as of truth. We live in a world in which things are not always just, for often the wicked prosper and the righteous suffer from exploitation.

For this reason it is important to recognize that God is innocent of the foolish and evil ways of men. We do not bow to the present and designate it as the kingdom of God. We do not abort the question of justice to make peace with the status quo. We hunger and thirst after righteousness, not from humility but because we are not satisfied with the world's present condition. Neither is God. With him we are in good company in our complaint, our efforts, and our patient insistence.

Stars in the sky, destiny, or common social arrangements, like habits in traditionalist tribal cultures, reproduce the same patterns from generation to generation. There is steadfastness, a security through anticipation and repetition. Yet repetition brings no respite and impersonal nature sheds no tears; nature's forces—divine or not—have no ears to hear and no power to act. Traditions' comfort is that they are faithful to the past and that they create a collective community of repeating motions and rituals. Whether god or the stars of the zodiac, whether Hegel's dialectic history or Mother Nature: all of life is already contained in a reality to be suffered or approved or exploited. It has always been this way. Any future is merely a repetition of the past.

A More Sensible and Satisfying Proposal

The Bible does not merely replace all these attachments with the word "God" laden with a tight sovereignty spin. The God of the Bible is not Allah of the Qur'an. A word "god" does not help us escape the tight and controlling net in which all religions catch humankind for the kill. Mere words like *god, sovereignty, will* and *permission* make no difference by themselves to the questions that our significant human reality poses. We require different answers in order for anything to be taken seriously under a moral and cultural evaluation.

What is so different in the Bible is the dynamic interplay between God and people through choices and consequences, by real personal actions and expressions of passion like pleasure and tears, involving both pleading and disappointment, and a flow of time. Creation, the Fall, the work of Christ on the cross in our past, and the Messiah walking down the street victoriously in a future time paint the canvas of a history in which we can really live, make choices, and complain. It is a true history of powerful interventions and purposeful activities and prophetic words. This is no play, no unrolling of a closed and determined program that may be sancti-fied in its orderliness but is intellectually and morally hollow.

The God of the Bible declares his choice to create and love human beings. When things went wrong through the disobedience of Adam and Eve, the rest of the Bible records how God runs after Adam and Eve and their children. His desire is that none be lost. He makes it possible to redeem them and his creation in nature by the free gift of pardon and the powerful victory of the resurrection. The reality of time and history is central to biblical thought. Only under the influence of Greek ideas in the church have they become curiously absent in some schools of theology. The component of God's patient, yet powerful battle for redemption is absent when everything has it rightful place already. Moral conflict, and with it the affirmation of a presently evil world, deserves a more biblical response than is found in the continuing discussion about the mo-rality of God and the historicity of true human existence.

The sensitive person must not be dropped between competing arguments. Bertrand Russell and the barber up the road, the dy-ing neighbor next door and the seeker burdened with an inhuman cultural-religious faith will find in the Bible the larger revelation of the gracious God and Father of Jesus Christ which he will often miss in church. Like any other gift offered to us, the unmerited fa-vor of God in Christ can then be first understood in its intellectual, moral, and historic context before being believed and accepted with "the empty hands of faith."